S.S.F. PUBLIC LIBRARY
WEST ORANGE AVENUE

SSF

S.S.F. PUBLIC LIBRARY
WEST ORANGE AVENUE

SEP   1998

THE WISDOM OF DEPRESSION

✦

616.8527
ZUE

THE WISDOM
of DEPRESSION

A Guide to
Understanding and Curing Depression
Using Natural Medicine

JONATHAN ZUESS, M.D.

HARMONY BOOKS
NEW YORK

S.S.F. PUBLIC LIBRARY
WEST ORANGE AVENUE

The author or his agents will not accept responsibility for injury, loss, or damage occasioned to any person acting or refraining from action as a result of material in this book whether or not such injury, loss, or damage is due in any way to any negligent act or omission, breach of duty, or default on the part of the author or his agents.

For the sake of privacy, the names of the patients whose stories are told in this book and the personal details that might identify them, have all been changed. In some examples, for the purpose of illustrating the use of different therapies, the stories of several different people were combined into a single story.

_____

Copyright © 1998 by Jonathan Zuess, M.D.

All rights reserved. No part of this book may be reproduced or transmitted in any form or by any means, electronic or mechanical, including photocopying, recording, or by any information storage and retrieval system, without permission in writing from the publisher.

Published by Harmony Books, a division of Crown Publishers, Inc., 201 East 50th Street, New York, New York, 10022 Member of the Crown Publishing Group.

Random House, Inc. New York, Toronto, London, Sydney, Auckland www.randomhouse.com

HARMONY and colophon are trademarks of Crown Publishers, Inc.

Printed in the United States of America

Design by Mary Jane DiMassi

Library of Congress Cataloging-in-Publication Data
Zuess, Jonathan.
The wisdom of depression : a guide to understanding
and curing depression using natural medicine / Jonathan G. Zuess. —
1st ed.
Includes bibliographical references.
(alk. paper)
1. Depression, Mental—Popular works.   2. Depression, Mental—
Alternative treatment.   I. Title.
RC537.Z85   1998
616.85'2706—dc21   97-30943

ISBN: 0-609-60108-3
10   9   8   7   6   5   4   3   2   1
First Edition

Dedicated to life!

ACKNOWLEDGMENTS

I owe the following people a debt of gratitude for their inspiration and support: Rabbi Zalman Schachter-Shalomi, Dr. Howard Silverman, Sarah Jane Freymann, Leslie Meredith, the staff of Glenside Hospital, Chantelle Brock for typing the manuscript, my whole family, and all of the people who have granted me the honor of traveling along with them for a while on their path of healing—you have all been my teachers.

CONTENTS

✦

and worked with the wisdom of her depressed response, it healed and enhanced her life as it was designed to do.

Andrea's Story

Andrea could not understand why she was feeling depressed—everything was going so well for her. A financially successful real estate agent in her late thirties, she had what most people would consider to be a very comfortable life. She was married to a caring and supportive man, and a nanny helped look after her two elementary school–aged children. She owned two houses and three cars. Her mother lived nearby, and they got along together well.

But somehow, sneaking up within her over the past few weeks was the suspicion that she was a failure. She was plagued with senseless, recurring thoughts that she was useless. At work, she felt unusually anxious in meetings—her heart would pound and her mouth would go dry. Social occasions, too, were becoming a kind of torture. She was respected for her success, but putting on a cheerful face was a strain, and she felt like a fraud.

She would lie awake at night worrying about trivial things. As she lay in the tangle of bedclothes, her mind paced restlessly through inner, winding corridors. And she dreamed:

> She stood barefoot on the cold cement floor in an aisle between rows of gleaming office furniture. She was in a large factory, and there was new-looking machinery in it. But it was strangely still and silent. There were no people there.

She woke feeling very disturbed. The next day, she was cranky and impatient from lack of sleep. The dream came back to her again the next night, and this time she woke up feeling exhausted. She canceled the appointments she had scheduled for that day and tried to get some rest.

CHAPTER 1

✦

HEALING TRANSFORMATIONS

What the caterpillar calls the end of the world, the master calls a butterfly.—RICHARD BACH

The secret of life is in the shadows and not in the open sun; to see anything at all, you must look deeply into the shadow of a living thing.
—UTE SAYING

It is the paradoxical secret of transformation itself, since it is in fact in and through the shadow that lead is transformed to gold.—CARL JUNG

DEPRESSION is a quest for vision; its essence is transformation. Depression wells up and encompasses us for a time in a state of painful, dream-saturated formlessness, but its true purpose is to provide the opportunity for healing insight, renewal, and reintegration.

Though we may not have recognized it, almost all of us have gone through this process, either partially or fully, several times in our lives. Most of us can think back to difficult times when we've lost a lot of sleep, felt irritable, and our appetite changed. Depression is one of the basic responses of human beings, produced when we encounter a difficult emotional challenge. As I'll show you, it is a natural and healthy response, and is actually specifically designed to help us deal with problems. It only becomes an illness if something goes badly wrong with it.

Consider the story of Andrea, a young woman who had come to a crisis point in her path. As you'll see, because she respected

3

✦

PART I

The Depressed Response: A Quest for Vision

In a dark time, the eye begins to see.
—*THEODORE ROETHKE*

tional medication for the treatment of mild-to-moderate depression, yet has only a small fraction of the side effects.

Throughout this book, you'll also find exercises that invite you to learn new skills—for example, relaxation and meditation techniques, exercises in creative thinking, and other self-help skills. You'll find guidelines, too, for the appropriate use of different types of therapies and medical services.

I'll share with you some of the stories of people who have used these and other treatments to overcome major depressive disorder. And I'll discuss the risks and benefits of conventional antidepressant medications. As a consumer, you deserve to be aware of the best options for your particular circumstances, regardless of which style of medicine your therapist practices.

If the process is respected and treated properly, depression can be a time of profound creativity and transformation. Time and again I have seen people emerge from it stronger, healthier, and more in touch with their wise inner self.

Although it challenges the traditional paradigm of depression, the message in this book is simple: It is about trusting in the wisdom of your own natural responses, and honoring your own innate capacity to grow and flourish.

becoming more and more ill. Major depressive disorder is definitely not a healthy process.

Why does this happen? What can go wrong with the
depressed response to stop it from resolving normally? As I
explain in Part II of this book, the response can be potentially
blocked or disrupted on any level—mental, physical, spiritual, or
social. These blockages interfere with your innate healing abilities and stop depression from resolving. I'll discuss the reasons
why this happens to so many people. As you'll see, factors like
poor nutrition and lack of exercise, being in a relationship where
you don't have the emotional space or safety to grow, an unrealistically negative style of thinking, and even physical illness can
interfere with the response and lead to major depressive disorder. We need to be functioning well on all levels for the response
to work properly.

When depression becomes an illness, you need help to
strengthen and support your healing capacities. A holistic treatment approach is best suited for this, since it nurtures all levels
of your being. In Part III I'll show you how you can use a holistic approach to heal major depressive disorder, incorporating the
best of both alternative and conventional medicine. Both styles
of medicine can complement each other. You'll learn how to create your own unique holistic plan, employing synergistic combinations of therapies addressing mind, body, and spirit.

You'll learn about new research findings into natural antidepressant approaches. For example, you may be surprised to
discover that sunlight therapy and certain nutritional supplements available in your local health-food store have proven to be
powerful medication in the treatment of major depressive disorder. As further examples, recent studies of exercise and meditation have also shown that they are effective in the prevention and
treatment of this condition. And exciting proof now exists that
the herb St. John's wort, used for thousands of years by the "wise
women" herbalists of Europe and Asia, is as effective as conven-

is often an essential step in the processes of creative problem solving and personal renewal. More than that, it is a type of basic response that is "built in" to the human organism for just those purposes.

In Part I of this book, I'll explain how the depressed response is a healing mechanism that has its origins in the deepest levels of the mind and body.[1] I'll also show how dreaming is a crucial part of the response.

Dreaming is a powerful problem-solving mode of the brain—it is a doorway into a healing realm. It brings you into contact with your most basic beliefs about the world and yourself. Scientific studies have shown that dreaming goes into high gear during depression. I'll show you how you can work with your dreams to increase their healing power.

The depressed response encompasses all levels of your being, including the spiritual. On this most profound of all levels, it is designed to emphasize your capacities for transcendence. I'll show you how it can enable you to see with your soul's vision, much like the vision-quests of Native American shamans. In the sacred dreamworld, the shamans undergo visionary transformative experiences. As you'll see, this dreamworld is also accessible to you.

You can further empower your depressed response through exercises to increase your creative problem-solving abilities. As I also describe in Part I, play, music, dance, art, and other forms of creativity can enhance your life in ways you may never have thought of.

But sometimes the depressed response does not succeed in its goal of inner transformation. The response can go wrong. Just as the immune response can sometimes go astray and turn into an autoimmune disorder, the depressed response can also sometimes turn into a serious illness, one that psychiatrists call "major depressive disorder." When this happens, instead of reaching a creative resolution, people become "stuck" in their depressions,

INTRODUCTION

✦

For nothing can be sole or whole
That has not been rent.
—WILLIAM BUTLER YEATS

There is wisdom to be found in depression. If we respect the process, it can teach us much about ourselves.

Through my work with hundreds of patients with depression, I have learned that there is much more to the condition than the conventional views can explain. It is *not* just a chemical imbalance in the brain. This book will present you with a new perspective, one that may surprise you. It will show you how depression can be a natural and healthy response, and how it is specially designed to enhance your abilities to overcome difficult emotional challenges. The response only becomes an illness if something goes seriously wrong with it.

When I graduated from medical school I shared the view of depression that is commonly held in our society—that it is always an illness. As I began to work with depressed people, though, I was struck by the way that a period of depression was often followed by a kind of personal renewal, a deep-seated transformation that enabled the individual to cope at a higher level than ever before. It seemed that sometimes breaking down was a necessary event for people, in that it allowed a truly meaningful reorganization and reintegration to occur on many levels of their lives.

Seeing the transformational and healing role that a period of depression can play, I have now come to believe—as do many psychotherapists and even some psychiatrists—that depression

AUTHOR'S NOTE

✦

The first part of this book discusses the depressed response, which, as I explain, is *not* the same as major depressive disorder. Major depressive disorder is covered in Parts 2 and 3. The symptoms of the two conditions are very similar: changes in mood, sleep, appetite, and so on, but a normal depressed response should last a maximum of around one week. *If symptoms of your depressed response go on for longer than a week, you should see a doctor immediately.* Your response may have gone astray and turned into major depressive disorder, which can be a very serious illness and should be treated medically. *If you are feeling suicidal at any time, see a doctor immediately.*

This book is designed to be used in conjunction with the care your doctor provides, thus giving you access to a comprehensive range of healing options. It is not intended for use as a substitute for consultation with a qualified medical practitioner. No book can provide the personalized care that you need.

You can read the chapters out of order, or in bits and pieces, choosing only those therapies that appeal to you. It's important to discuss them first with your doctor, so that he or she can help tailor your therapy specifically for you. Most of the therapies can be used alongside conventional medication if you wish, with the exception of St. John's wort (described in Chapter 11) and amino acid supplements (see Chapter 12).

I encourage you to explore, experiment, and find out what works best in your life. You are unique, and the answers that are right for you are unlike anyone else's. Allow yourself to be creative—the essence of healing is creativity.

Once the children were off to school, she sat in bed, day-dreamed, and wrote in her journal. As she mulled over the dream, she realized that the furniture reminded her of her father's office, which she had visited as a child. It was at the time when he had been promoted to division manager in the large company he worked for. She remembered that visit well, since it was the last time she'd seen him at work. A few months after his promotion, he was killed in a car accident.

Suddenly her dream made sense to her: the shiny office furniture and the eerie absence of people. She understood that as a child she had connected the two events in her mind—her father's shining success at the office and his tragic death. *Success is dangerous,* the dream was telling her; *no one can remain there.* And as she thought about it now, she felt a sudden stab of anger at her father for having been at work, away from her for so much of his time, and for having been so successful.

On a subconscious level now, she understood that her own success in business also felt dangerous to her. Her heart had been trying to tell her this as it pounded in her chest during meetings. These vague feelings were compounded by her nagging worries that she was neglecting her children because of her work schedule. The real danger of success in work, she realized, was that it can take you away from your children—as it had done with her father.

This complex mixture of issues—unresolved grief, negative beliefs from her childhood, and a desire to spend more time with her children—had been partly submerged in her unconscious mind. Her symptoms of depression had been a sign that her mind and body were struggling to resolve the conflict. Because she was willing to pay attention to her dreams, the issues had been brought to light. Now she was able to add the resources of her conscious mind to deal with them.

Andrea decided to cut down her work hours, from her previous sixty or sixty-five hours per week to a more reasonable forty. She accomplished this by taking on an associate. This improved her lifestyle tremendously; with her associate covering much of the after-hours work, Andrea had more time for her children and partner. She was also able to set aside time for herself for a daily morning walk.

Within a very short time Andrea experienced a dramatic improvement in her mood. She felt that for the first time in her life she was fully actualizing her priorities. For her, the depressed response had been an important step in the process of her self's unfolding.

As you'll discover in this book, stories like hers are not rare. If the depressed response is respected, and treated properly, they are more the rule than the exception.

Our Bodymind's Healing Responses

Every disease is a physician.—IRISH PROVERB

We usually think of our body and mind as somehow being independent of each other. The truth is that they are so *inter*-dependent that they might really just be different ways of describing the same thing. I like to refer to them with a single term, the bodymind, because it expresses their essential oneness.

The human bodymind has a profound ability to heal itself. Over the millennia of evolution, built-in healing mechanisms have been developed to protect us from all sorts of problems: infections, poisons, physical trauma, and even psychological difficulties. When these healing mechanisms are activated, they cause major changes in our bodymind, changes that are designed to help us overcome or adapt to problems. Many things can be altered: the functioning of our cells and organs, the level of hormones, the body's temperature, the amount of energy we feel, the sleep/wake cycle, and even our mood.

But these healing changes in themselves can be distressing. In fact, most of the symptoms of illness that we experience are actually produced by our bodymind as it struggles to deal with and overcome the underlying problems.

Consider the following example: You unknowingly ate a toxic substance. Your bodymind would then respond with changes specifically designed to overcome the effect of the toxin. Your brain's built-in vomiting centers would be activated, causing nausea and vomiting in order to expel the toxin. You would also lose your appetite, encouraging you to rest your bowels and allowing you to recover. Your healing responses would thus be acting wisely to overcome the problem, even though all that you might be conscious of is that you're feeling very sick and distressed. You might mistakenly think that your vomiting is itself the problem rather than the solution.

Another example: You were exposed to a flu virus. Your bodymind would respond with changes specifically designed to enhance your ability to fight the infection. Your brain's built-in fever center would be activated—raising your body temperature so that your immune system could work more efficiently. Your immune cells would release large amounts of interferon, a chemical that is antiviral but also causes muscle aching and tiredness. Those unpleasant side effects are meant to encourage you to rest and conserve your strength for the fight against the virus. You might mistakenly think that your problem is just that you have a fever, muscle aches, and feel tired. In fact, those symptoms are caused by your body's healing forces in action—they are the solution, not the problem.

Now let's consider the example of when you are consciously or unconsciously facing a difficult emotional situation in your life, one that you are unable to resolve through normal, everyday means. Your bodymind would then respond with changes specifically designed to enhance your ability to do inner work and to create a solution to the crisis. Certain areas in your brain and endocrine system would become activated, causing changes in your emotional and physical functioning. You would become fatigued and irritable, symptoms that are intended to encourage you to take a break from your other activities and to spend some time on your own. Your mind would become preoccupied with the problem, searching for all possible solutions. Your appetite and sleep would usually diminish, thus allowing you to focus on your inner work, and feelings of profound dissatisfaction and restlessness would occur in order to motivate you to continue this work.

The work of internal creativity and transformation could then take place through soul-searching self-examination, the consideration of radical changes, and intense, restless dreaming. Finally, having gone through this painful and distressing process, you would emerge from it stronger than before. You would have had a kind of rebirth, a healing crisis.

Like the immune response or the vomiting response, the depressed response is "built in" to the human system and is designed to help you overcome problems. As in the cases of those other responses, you might not be conscious of the underlying problem. In fact, at least some part of the problem is usually below the level of awareness, in your subconscious mind. There are almost always some subconscious conflicts going on, struggling to be solved—just as in Andrea's case. This is the reason why all levels of your being are activated, including your subconscious mind and your body. And that's also why dreams play such an important role in the depressed response, as I'll discuss in the next chapter.

Because you are not fully aware of the underlying problem, however, you can mistakenly believe that the only thing wrong with you is that you have the symptoms of depression, whereas those symptoms are actually part of the solution. As in many of the conditions we call illness, the symptoms are actually caused by your own protective healing forces in action.

Your bodymind has its own wisdom. All you really need to do is cooperate with it.

Why Conventional Medicine
Falls Short of Healing Us

*The natural healing force within each of us is the greatest
force in getting well.*—HIPPOCRATES

Conventionally trained physicians lack trust in our innate healing mechanisms. They prefer to use therapies that suppress
symptoms and block or override the healing response. If you go
to a conventional doctor to be treated for a flu, for instance, the
doctor would likely recommend a drug like aspirin or acetaminophen. These drugs suppress your immune response—
interfering with the activity of the fever-center in your brain and
stopping the production of interferon. Your temperature would
then fall, and your muscle aches and tiredness would diminish.
The distressing symptoms of the healing crisis would be suppressed, and you would feel better in the short term, but your
healing would be counteracted. In fact, recent clinical research
has shown that drugs that block the immune response—aspirin
and acetaminophen—actually worsen viral infections, allowing
viruses to multiply more rapidly and increasing the duration of
the illness.[1] In addition, because these drugs weaken your
immune system, you form fewer protective antibodies, making
you more susceptible to future infections.

In a similar way, many conventional physicians prescribe
sedatives and/or antidepressants to people who are undergoing
a normal depressed response. These drugs suppress the process.
They diminish your ability to concentrate and conduct mental
and emotional work. Drugs also interfere with the important
problem-solving process of dreaming. As a result, the stage of
creative emotional reintegration may be slowed—and in some
cases it may not occur at all. If that happens, rather than emerging stronger from the response, you would be emotionally
weaker and more susceptible to further episodes of depression.

I should add here that if the depressed response has for whatever reason failed to resolve properly, and gone on to become an unproductive case of major depressive disorder, these medications may be necessary to break the cycle of illness. But like other physicians who practice natural medicine, I much prefer to use therapies that enhance and support, rather than suppress, healing responses. By encouraging your innate healing mechanisms to operate, you are able to achieve a higher, more complete state of well-being than before—and that is the essence of good health care.

Enhancing Your Healing Response

The physician is only Nature's assistant.—GALEN

For Nature ever faithful is
To such as trust her faithfulness.
—RALPH WALDO EMERSON

If you went to a practitioner of natural medicine for a flu, in contrast to a conventional physician, he or she would recommend using nutrients and herbs that enhance your immune response—like vitamin C and A, and the immunostimulant herb Echinacea. The practitioner would also recommend simple rest to support your immune functioning. Once your immune response had resolved itself naturally, you would then be stronger and better adapted than before, since you would have produced additional protective antibodies.

In a similar way, the natural treatment of your depressed response would also be supportive, aimed at cooperating with your bodymind's efforts. A brief time off from work, rest, and allowing yourself to dream restlessly may be all that you need. With the successful resolution of your depressed response, as with your immune response, you would also be stronger and better adapted than before.

On the other hand, if your depressed response failed to resolve normally within a reasonable length of time—say, a week or so—it had probably become the unproductive, self-perpetuating state known as major depressive disorder, and should be treated as an illness. In that case, the natural approach to your treatment would be more active, aimed at correcting any blockages that might exist to your own healing efforts—psychological, physical, and spiritual—and providing the best conditions for them to operate.

As I'll show later, dream analysis, psychological therapies aimed at identifying and changing unrealistic negative thoughts, the learning of coping skills, and other ways of consciously enhancing the creative problem-solving process, would be supplemented with a relaxation and meditation program. These would be integrated with physical therapies involving diet, nutritional supplementation, exercise, and sunlight therapy. The herbal medication St. John's wort could also be used, since it acts in harmony with natural processes. It has been proven to be as effective as conventional medication for the treatment of mild to moderate depression, but unlike them, it is nonsedating and actually improves information processing by your brain.[2] St. John's wort also does not interfere with the process of dreaming, as most antidepressant drugs do.[3]

Would you need a conventional antidepressant drug? It would depend on how severe your depression is. Because I am aware of the many safe and effective treatments for mild cases of major depressive disorder, I reserve conventional antidepressant medication for people with moderate to severe depression. For mild cases, supportive natural therapies allow the patient's own internal healing processes to function best. The drive for creative reintegration, arising from deep within the vital forces, is nurtured rather than stifled.

To illustrate how a holistic approach can help, let me relate the story of Greg, whose depressed response had become chronic and had turned into a mild case of major depressive disorder.

Greg's Story

Life had been unfair to Greg, there was no doubt about it. He was twenty-seven years old and in his second year of an architecture course. He was also profoundly deaf, and because of this his studies were extremely difficult for him. He could lip-read, but if his lecturers turned to write on the board, or if they had strong accents, he would miss what they were saying. He had tried to keep up with the rest of the class by copying other students' notes, doing additional reading, and requesting extra tutorials, and so he had managed to struggle through the first year. The second year, though, was proving to be more than he could handle. One class in particular, involving difficult concepts in materials technology, had really brought things to a head.

The professor had such a heavy accent that Greg could understand only a few words each lecture. He had asked to be reassigned to another lecture stream, but when he was, he found things were no better. His new teacher was heavily bearded and mumbled. Additional tutorials and reading were of limited help to Greg, since he also had difficulties with the math involved.

Feelings of frustration and anger were beginning to overwhelm him. The current problems in his class only seemed to highlight his pain at the unfairness of being born deaf into a hearing world. Actually, those feelings had always been there, but he had grown up in a family that was heavily invested in the Anglo-Saxon traditions that frowned on discussing one's troubles. Men, especially, had to keep a stiff upper lip—anything else was considered a display of weakness. So he suppressed his feelings and soldiered on.

But gradually building up over a period of about a month and a half, the symptoms of depression had started to impair Greg's ability to study. He couldn't concentrate and had lost his appetite. He would stay up late into the night studying, and even though he felt exhausted, he would only be able to sleep for a few hours at a time. Midterm exams were approaching, and he had started to use alcohol to control his anxious, jumpy feelings. He felt so stressed that he worried that he might be losing his mind.

He first came to see me with a request for some tablets to help him sleep. As we talked about what was happening in his life, his barely contained despair was evident. Emotionally, he was like a dam on the verge of bursting.

Clearly, there were several areas in his life that needed therapeutic attention. We talked about what he might do to help cope with his difficult circumstances.

First, to be able to deal with the underlying problems, he needed to take better care of himself physically. He recognized the detrimental effects of alcohol, so fortunately he was quite willing to stop using it. I prescribed St. John's wort for him, and as a student he appreciated the fact that rather than making him feel fuzzy-headed like most other antidepressants, it actually improved his ability to think clearly. He also took supplemental vitamins and minerals and returned to the soccer training he had quit the year before. He found that this gave him more energy and helped him to sleep better—more than making up for the time it took out of his schedule.

We explored the options that remained for dealing with his studies. He went to the university's disabilities liaison officer, but she felt she had done all she could to help Greg. There were no other lecturers to whom he could be assigned. She would not provide funds for a note-taker to be hired, saying the university couldn't afford it.

Greg eventually went to the Equal Opportunities Commission, who worked out a deal for the university to provide a Dictaphone and transcription service for the lectures. With determined hard work, he passed the exam and continued on with his studies.

In the meantime, though, Greg also received counseling.

Using his dreams as a starting point, we worked on issues relating to expressing rather than suppressing his feelings. He discovered that rather than being a sign of weakness, expressing yourself required courage. Other issues related to this were also dealt with, such as his contempt for people whom he felt were weak. He came to the insight that this contempt was actually directed mainly at himself; he looked upon his deafness as a personal weakness and had never been able to accept himself for it. This realization was the beginning of his process of self-acceptance.

For Greg, the difficulties in his studies had brought out inner conflicts that had been suppressed for years. His depression was a reflection of the need to come to a new understanding and a new way of dealing with things. His depressed response had became chronic, probably for a number of reasons: the suppression of his feelings, his abuse of alcohol, and also the severity of the difficulties he was experiencing in his life. Still, he was able to overcome his major depressive disorder and make the necessary transitions in his life.

Finding Your Own Wisdom

*Like an ability or muscle, hearing your inner wisdom is
strengthened by doing it.*—ROBBIE GASS

It can be hard to trust your natural responses, especially when they are themselves painful and disorienting. But as in Greg's and Andrea's cases, depression can actually be an essential part of your own processes of inner reevaluation, problem solving, and renewal. The source of your depressed response is the flow of creative life-energy arising from deep within you. Through it, you can find your own wisdom—and move beyond depression to start enjoying life again.

In the following chapters, we'll look at specific ways in which you can cooperate with and enhance your own innate healing abilities. The whole idea is about having trust in yourself and respecting your own capacities. And it's also quite literally about following your dreams.

CHAPTER 2

✦

DREAMS

The dream is the small hidden door in the deepest and
most intimate sanctum of the soul.—CARL JUNG

The dreamer's world is also the shaman's world. It is a
world . . . that constitutes itself around the heart of
a sacred mystery.—LEE IRWIN

THERE is a world within the one we know, a world that exists
within the same place and time but is connected to ours only
by the most slender and subtle of paths. It is the world of dreams.
When we are depressed we travel the path that leads us there.
And that is the path of healing.

Dreams hold the key to depression. Even more than that,
they are crucial to us as human beings—emotionally, biologically, and spiritually. We literally could not exist without them.

But before I explain this, let's take a journey into the dreamworld for a few moments. Our guides for now will be the
shamans of the Native American peoples. During their vision-
quests, the shamans live dreams as reality. After preparing themselves by going off into isolation in the wilderness, where they
fast and meditate, they cross into the sacred realm of dreams.
There they find healing powers and undergo transformations.
What happens there is as real to them as their experiences in the
realm of ordinary consciousness, because the two realms are
blended seamlessly together in their spiritual universe.

Pretty Shield, an Absarokee medicine woman, gave this
account of the vision-quest she undertook after the death of her
infant daughter, around the year 1930:

16

I had slept little, sometimes lying down alone in the hills at night. . . . I ate only enough to keep me alive, hoping for a medicine-dream, a vision, that would help me to live and to help others. One morning . . . I saw a woman ahead of me. . . . I saw that she was not a real woman, but that she was a [sacred] Person, and that she was standing beside an ant hill. . . . "Rake up the side of this ant hill and ask for the things that you wish, daughter," the Person said, and then she was gone.

Now in this medicine-dream, I entered a beautiful white lodge, with a war-eagle at the head. He did not speak to me, and yet I have often seen him since that day. And even now the ants help me. I listen to them always. They are my medicine. . . .[1]

Through this dream, Pretty Shield encountered an intuitive natural wisdom that healed her and gave her the ability to heal others. Around the same time, an Omaha man also told of his vision-quest, in which he experienced a kind of transformation and cleansing:

He came to the hilltop. . . . He scooped a bedding place in a bank of soft earth to sleep in. He slept by day and watched by night, and cried to Wakonda at sun-up. . . . The fourth day the sun came up with a thick fog so he could not see. . . . Then the fog lifted for a moment and he saw through it a figure as large as a man standing but looking like an owl, and lots of small owls of common size flying over its head. A wind of fog whirled over him and covered him like smoke. His body felt like it was being turned inside out . . . leaving it clean like.[2]

Both anthropologists and shamans agree that the remarkable experiences that occur during vision-quests happen in a type of vivid dream state.[3] Actually, the search for personal empowerment through dreams is one of the central features of Native

American Plains religions. Far from considering dreams to be mere nonsense, as western culture often sees them, the Native Americans respect and cherish them as a sacred means of healing.

Dreams Heal Us

It is not only shamans who enter the dreamworld to find transformative and healing powers. We all do it. Our dreams keep us healthy; they keep us sane; they are the foundation that holds up the rest of our being. Dreaming is a time of emotionally processing and integrating all of the things that happen to us during waking hours. The type of brain waves produced during dreaming—beta waves—are also found during waking periods when people are involved in complex learning tasks. Dreaming is a special mode of the brain designed for intensive problem solving.

Studies have shown that people who have had traumatic experiences, or are under stress, or are in difficult learning situations spend more time in the dreaming state—they need the extra dreams to help them cope. If people are deprived of their dreams by waking them every time they enter the rapid eye movement (REM) phase of sleep (when most dreaming occurs), they become seriously unwell. They become anxious, irritable, unable to concentrate, and depressed. They may even begin to hallucinate—a kind of spillover of dreams into the waking state. As soon as they're allowed to sleep normally again, they spend extra time in the REM state, to make up for what they've lost.

These sorts of observations have led scientists to conclude that dreams are so important that they might be the main reason people need to sleep at all.[4] They also suggest that there are very strong links between dreaming and the state of depression.

Why Dreams Hold the Key to Depression

In the late seventies, Harvey Fiss and his colleagues, a group of clinical researchers at the University of Connecticut School of Medicine, decided to examine the therapeutic power of dreams in a systematic way. They took patients who were undergoing conventional psychotherapy for depression but who had, according to their therapists, been unable to make any further progress. They were then taken through a two-week-long series of exercises the psychologists called "Dream Enhancement Therapy." The purpose of the therapy was essentially to immerse the patients in their dreams. It was an intensive program of recording and then working through their dreams, taking seriously their dreams' symbolic language. After this two-week program, these patients were found to have all experienced a marked improvement in their depression, anxiety, feelings of inadequacy, and low self-esteem.[5]

How could this happen? Somehow, something very significant was going on in these people's dreams—something that needed to be acknowledged and respected.

In fact, we know that dreams are more crucial to people when they're feeling depressed than at any other time. In sleep laboratories it's been found that depressed people spend almost twice the percentage of their sleep time dreaming than other people do. They also enter the dream state very rapidly after falling asleep, which is unusual, since this normally takes quite a while. Depressed people do very hard work in their dreams and often wake up exhausted as a result.

With these scientific findings in mind, let's go back for a moment and look at the rituals of the shamans. Throughout most Native American cultures, there are three main conditions through which powerful healing dreams are obtained: isolation, fasting, and meditation.[6] These conditions sound strangely familiar. Interestingly, they are exactly the conditions that the depressed response encourages in us. We want to be alone (isolation), we lose our appetite (fasting), and we become inwardly focused and preoccupied (meditation). And all of this leads us on an intense and exhausting journey into the world of dreams—the same path the shamans take. There, in the dreamworld, we are able to undergo healing transformations.

The depressed response occurs because of our deep, biologically driven need for a vision-quest. We could even call it the "visionquest response." In times of trouble, it wells forth from the depths of our bodymind, granting us access to the world of primal symbols. It is our means of venturing into the sacred dreamworld of the shamans.

As the study at the University of Connecticut shows, for our vision-quest/depressed response to succeed fully, we need to consciously acknowledge and respect it. We need to understand that it is in the unmapped depths of our being that our strength is born and renewed. We need to take our dreams seriously, to cooperate with the wisdom that is embedded within our spiritual and biological self.

Evolving Through Dreams

Dreams are such an important part of who we are that without them we would probably never have evolved! In his book *Brain and Psyche: The Biology of the Unconscious,* neuroscientist Dr. Jonathan Winson describes how we owe our very existence to our capacity to dream.[7] It seems that REM sleep was an adaptation made by the early mammals; lower orders of animals, like reptiles and monotremes, do not have it. Monotremes are creatures like the echidna and platypus; they lay eggs but are warm-blooded and milk-producing—a midway step between reptiles and mammals.

Dr. Winson points out that as you advance up the phylogenetic tree of species, the size of the animals' prefrontal cortex

increases. This is the area of the brain devoted to overall order-
ing and integration of thought, and its size corresponds best with
what we call intelligence. But there is an odd discontinuity in its
steady growth as you ascend evolutionarily, from reptiles to
monotremes to mammals. At the step up from the monotremes,
like the echidna, to such mammals as the rat, the prefrontal cortex shrinks back down again, so that it is much smaller in the rat
than in those lower orders. And yet the rat is *much* cleverer than
anything below it on the evolutionary tree. Even the echidna,
which has a huge prefrontal cortex—larger in relative terms than
that of any other creature, including humans—is very unintelli-
gent compared with the rat and other mammals. Somehow the
mammals discovered a way to make much more efficient use of
their prefrontal cortex.

Dr. Winson believes it was the development of REM sleep
and dreaming that enabled mammals to do this. Rather than
having to process and integrate new experiences as they happened during the day, mammals developed the ability to store
the experiences temporarily during the day, and then switch
into a special processing/integrating mode at night—REM
sleep. This freed their prefrontal cortex from having to work so
hard during the day, and therefore it could be much smaller. If
not for our ability to dream, says Dr. Winson, we would simply
never have been able to evolve—our prefrontal cortexes would
have had to be so large that we'd have to carry them around in
wheelbarrows!

So it is our dreams that have allowed us to develop and
become who we are. Let's look more closely at how this extraordinary ability of ours works.

REM Sleep and Symbols

There are two basic kinds of dreams, which correspond to the
two basic phases of sleep: REM and non-REM.

Almost all dreams occur in the REM sleep phase. In REM sleep, your entire being is focused on an emotional/subconscious level. It is as though you abandon your physical body. Your muscles are paralyzed, except for the muscles controlling eye movements, which are highly active, as though intently watching the dream dramas unfold. Your brain is highly active during REM sleep; often more active than during waking hours. The dreams that occur during this time tend to have a surrealistic quality—full of symbolic imagery and half-glimpsed meanings.

Freud believed that the dreaming mind used symbols because they were less threatening to the ego than the things they were meant to represent. For example, a person might dream about a hat in order to conceal the true subject, which, Freud believed, was usually something related to sex. Modern psychologists, however, have found ample evidence that the mind uses symbols not to conceal but to *reveal* deeper meanings and the connections between things. A hat, for example, can in a single symbol represent a situation that is "on one's mind," is important for protection in some way, is related to being outdoors or to a particular profession, that can be left behind by accident, and so on. A multitude of meanings can be condensed into one symbol, weaving together many points in the vast web of an individual's consciousness. It makes sense, then, that each individual's dream symbols are unique. No one else has access to quite the same tapestry of experience.

That is why the healing dreams that people in our culture experience are not likely to feature the same types of symbols as the dreams of the shamans. But ours can be just as profound, containing our own powerful images.

The symbol-filled realm of REM sleep lies fairly close to the surface of your consciousness. You can easily be woken out of it and remember what happened there. In non-REM sleep, though, you go much deeper into the unconscious realm. Here your entire being is focused on the physical level. Your brain is less active, but your body is no longer immobile and shifts position frequently.

Metabolic processes of physical regeneration and repair go into high gear. In a sense, in non-REM sleep, you ground yourself in your physical reality, and your vital force is renewed.

It is more difficult to wake someone during non-REM sleep, and if woken, a person usually remains groggy and confused for a few minutes. Dreams are rare in this sleep phase. It may just be, though, that it is more difficult to remember them, since your awareness must travel a greater distance up out of non-REM sleep to the waking state.

The dreams of non-REM sleep, however, can be extraordinary. They are the ones that are so lucid and realistic that you are not sure if you are dreaming or awake. Sometimes you feel as if you're just lying there, awake, when you're actually deeply unconscious. Sometimes there's a heightened sense of reality in these dreams; as though they were more real than the waking state. And in some rare cases, you're left with the feeling that some great truth has been revealed, as though some aspect of your soul or its mission has been made known to you.

These sorts of dreams can have a profound effect on your life. They are a point of contact with your own most basic beliefs about yourself and the world, and they can be exceptionally useful to work with. Almost all psychotherapists agree that any kind of dream can teach you much about yourself if you let it.

Dreams as Messages

Thus, learning to understand our dreams is a matter of learning to understand our heart's language.
— ANN FARADAY

The Talmud, a vast compilation of ancient Jewish teachings, contains several interesting discussions on dreams. It was believed that dreams could convey messages from higher spiritual realms, but that the active imagination of the dreamer introduced distortions into these messages. As a result, all dreams contained at least some small portion that had no validity. Dreams about demons, for example, were by definition false.

Dreams were also described as "unread letters," in that if they were ignored, their messages had no ability to affect waking reality. If the messages were taken seriously, they could be interpreted in many different ways, and all of them could be equally true, providing that the interpreter had the ability to see through the dream's distortions. (This seems to agree with modern psychological analyses of the function of dream symbols as being to condense many different meanings into one object.) An example is given of a man who consulted twenty-four dream interpreters, each of whom gave a different explanation of his dream; and yet, all of them came true.[8]

Later Jewish mystical sources added that further pointers to a dream's validity were its clearness and vividness.[9] Native American shamans say very similar things about important dreams. Lame Deer (John Fire) of the Lakota Sioux, for instance, said: "The real vision . . . is very real. It hits you sharp and clear like an electric shock. . . . You have to work for this, empty your mind for it."[10]

The shamans also say that the more serious the problem for which you are seeking to find healing in the medicine dream, the more preparation is required. Purification ceremonies such as sweats (a sort of ritual sauna) are usually performed, as well as earnest prayer and meditation.[11] When this kind of preparation is done, people are empowered to obtain dreams that come from the deepest levels of their soul.

Edward's Dream Vision

Edward was at a low point in his life. His job of managing a busy retail franchise was proving to be more than he could handle. He dreamed:

*I was walking up flights of stairs, in a stairwell without doors
that seemed to go on forever. Finally I reached the top. There
were solid walls all around me, but the roof was open to the sky.
I looked up, and there wasn't really a sky—just an emptiness
that went on up into heaven. A feeling seemed to penetrate me:
I became aware that I was being watched by God. There were
no words, just an indescribable feeling.*
 I still think about this dream, and it helps me.

How Dreams Help Us During Depression

Recent dream research stops short of calling dreams messages
from the spiritual realm, but it does indeed suggest that dreams
put us in touch with our deepest, and sometimes entirely unconscious, beliefs about the world. The research findings have led us
to piece together how dreams help us during depression.

It's been discovered, for example, that depressed people not
only spend more time dreaming, they also spend more time than
average dreaming about their past. Their dreams contain more
childhood elements, and more family members. The dreams of
severely depressed people also tend to be filled with hostile and
threatening themes.[12]

Another particularly fascinating piece of information has
emerged from the research: If you stop people who are *severely*
depressed from dreaming, they get better. In fact, this is considered to be how most synthetic antidepressant drugs work—by
suppressing REM sleep, the main dreaming stage. They simply
stop you from dreaming normally, or at least interfere with the
process.[13] (St. John's wort, the herbal antidepressant discussed in
Chapter 11, does not do this; it works through different means.)[14]

People who are *mildly* depressed (who constitute the majority of depressed people and who include people who are having
a depressed response), on the other hand, tend to feel *worse* if
deprived of their REM sleep, just like nondepressed people.

How can we explain these confusing observations? First of all, it's clear that depression is a state where a person is confronted by some problem that severely strains the usual methods of problem solving. Since dreaming is one of the main means of problem solving, it goes into high gear.

In dreams, a person attempts to arrive at some sort of emotional solution to a current situation, using the basic system of beliefs that were formed in the past. This explains why the past features so strongly in the dreams of depressed people.

For the majority of people with depression, the dreaming process is at least partly effective at helping them cope. This is why these people are only mildly depressed, and it's also why they feel worse if deprived of their dreams.

But if a person's basic beliefs about the world are that it is a hostile, threatening place, that person is only going to become more depressed when he dreams. This is what happens in the case of severely depressed people. In their dreams, they go back to their beliefs about how bad the world is, and so they end up feeling worse.

Their negative beliefs from the past are not only stopping them from getting better, they're often what led them to becoming depressed in the first place. And that is why cutting them off from their past by stopping them from dreaming makes them feel better. Antidepressant medication helps them by partially blocking the pain of the past.

That pain and those beliefs remain, though, unless conscious efforts are made to heal them, which is why many people with major depressive disorder who have not had some sort of psychotherapy have a relapse when they stop their medication.

The good news is that you can heal even the most deeply rooted negative beliefs from your past. One of the ways you can do this is through working consciously with your dreams, as the people in the University of Connecticut study did. You will have the added benefit of using your conscious mind along with your unconscious; it's like having twice the power available to you.

The improvements you will feel are all the more significant because, unlike with the use of drugs, you will not be suppressing your dreams and unconscious belief systems. Instead, you will be actively reintegrating your dreams with the help of your conscious mind. Real healing can occur, not just the suppression of symptoms.

Let me relate Nancy's story to show how you can begin this healing work.

Nancy's Story

When Nancy thought back to her childhood, some of her most prominent memories were of the times when her mother was in the hospital. Her mother, it seemed, went there quite often, and sometimes stayed for months at a time. Only in her late teen years did Nancy learn that her mother's illness had actually been recurrent major depressive disorder. Now Nancy was thirty-five years old, with a little girl of her own, and was afraid she would end up the same way.

In therapy, she discussed her dreamworld. She had dreamed:

I was on the deck of a cruise ship, moving slowly upstream on a river that wound through a canyon. I felt the engine chugging and straining. Black smoke flowed from the stacks. In my hand was a framed photograph of myself and my brother. My hand felt very tired; I couldn't move it. There were orange flowers growing in boxes on the deck.

In this dream, Nancy saw images that represented her own personality: the black flowing smoke was like her hair; the straining engines represented her struggle. But she realized that the hand holding the photograph was her mother's, and the flower boxes were like the ones her mother used to keep. The images representing her were blended with those representing her mother.

Through decoding and discussing that dream and others like it, Nancy came to redefine her issue as being a fear that she was in fact just an extension of her mother and not an independent personality. She understood then that the real task she needed to begin—as with so many other people in this world—was to learn how to respect her own uniqueness. Her dream insight gave her a conscious goal to work toward in her therapy and in the rest of her life.

Enhancing the Healing Power of Your Dreams

Realistic people with practical aims are rarely as realistic and practical in the long run of things as the dreamers who pursue their dreams.—HANS SELYE

To honor your vision-quest response, you need to take seriously the insights your dreams provide for you. I have based the following program on the Dream Enhancement Therapy described earlier.[15] You will need a pen, notepad and/or blank journal, flashlight or other dim source of light, and art materials.

Step 1. Direct your dreams   Before going to sleep, pick a specific problem you are having. Then suggest a possible solution to it. Repeat this suggestion several times before falling asleep. In other words, you are trying to focus on solutions here, to get your brain into "solutions-mode."

Step 2. Record your dreams   Keep a pen, notepad, and flashlight next to your bed. When you wake up in the morning or at any time during the night, quickly write down as much of the dream as you are able to recall. (*Note:* If your dream was a severe nightmare, you might be better off not working with it. Extremely terrifying dreams may be too difficult to work with when you're feeling fragile. Focus on your other dreams for the time being.)

Step 3. Work consciously with your dreams For each dream, devote a page in your journal to answering the following questions:

- What does this dream mean to you?
- What does it reveal about you as a person?
- Does it help you understand or solve your problem? And if so, how?
- Does it identify a new problem for you?
- If it doesn't solve the problem, how would you solve it?

Step 4. Visualize the solution Do this with the same sort of symbols you encountered in the dream. This is an important element, since it helps to transmute conscious thoughts into the language of the subconscious mind. For example, if, in your dream, you were on board a hot-air balloon during a storm, visualize a scene where the winds and rain abate, and you float gently back home.

I encourage you also to preserve your dreams and your visualized solutions in drawings or paintings, and to continue to reflect on them throughout the day.

How to Bring on a Powerful Dream

Like the shamans, you can take some specific steps to bring on a powerful dream. The most important thing is to respect your vision-quest/depressed response when it comes to you. You don't need to go out in the wilderness and fast for four days. But you can take a few days off from your normal routine to be alone. If your appetite is poor, respect that and eat little. Lie in bed and allow yourself to daydream. Meditate and pray for a medicine dream. (*Please note:* If the symptoms of your depressed response last longer than a week, or if you are feeling suicidal, see a doctor immediately.)

To have a vivid dream, set your alarm clock to wake you an hour or two earlier than your usual time. On waking, shower and put on clean, loose-fitting clothes. Then meditate and pray for twenty minutes, and then lie back down. If you sleep again, you will dream vividly. This is because REM sleep periods are more common during the early morning hours. By waking up and then going back to sleep, you bring your conscious awareness into closer contact with your REM periods. You thereby increase your degree of immersion into the dreamworld.

In fact, this sort of interrupted sleep in the early morning often occurs naturally during the depressed response, as well as during major depressive disorder. Psychiatrists refer to the phenomenon as "early morning wakening," though they have no explanation as to why it occurs.

Decoding Your Dreams

The recent event transformed into imagery is the bridge into the dream, just as the pictorial narrative transformed into a verbal report is the bridge out of it. The moment we learn to walk the bridge, our lives can come full circle. —JAN TOLAAS

Dreams are often difficult for the conscious mind to interpret. Among Native Americans, too, dreams can sometimes be vague, and require much thought and discussion with advisers in order to be understood. Here are some tips to help decode your dreams.

- Take each dream symbol, element, or action separately. Write down a list of all your past associations with it, using as much lateral thinking as you can. You will know the correct answer when you find it because it will intuitively feel right.

- If its meaning still eludes you, try a method of projective association: Take a book or some other item that has power for you. You might use a Bible, I Ching, or other spiritual text, runes or other such tokens or cards. Open the book at random, or do a random pick of the cards or tokens. Take the sections of the book you've opened to or the spread of cards and read it; try to find some associations from it to your dream. In other words, you are projecting your dream onto its structure to see if any shared patterns exist. If your first reading is not satisfactory, try another.
- If projective association methods are inadequate, look for a book on dream interpretation at your local library. Remember that they can only suggest *possible* answers— you alone will be able to tell if they are correct or not, because every individual's dream symbols are unique. It's also true, though, that there may be some archetypal symbols that we all use.
- And finally, I should mention the most obvious source of help in dream interpretation: your therapist. Nearly all therapists, regardless of their style, see the value of interpreting and working with dreams.

Venturing into the Sacred

Healing proceeds from the depths to the heights.
—CARL JUNG

The shamans know that at our core is holiness. This is why they consider sacred rituals to be such an important part of the quest for healing dreams. Rituals, especially prayer and meditation, attune you to the depths that you must traverse in your journey. They can greatly empower your quest for vision and help you obtain a medicine dream. In the next chapter, we'll consider some of the spiritual aspects of the depressed response.

CHAPTER 3

✦

THE SOUL'S VISION

*Sacred space and sacred time and something joyous to do
is all we need. Almost anything then becomes a continuous and increasing joy.*—JOSEPH CAMPBELL

*There is no man who is not incessantly being taught by
his soul.*—RABBI PINCHAS OF KORETZ, c. 1780

The Soul Experience of Depression

D O our souls experience our depressions? Are they involved
in them in any way? Or are they entirely free of limitations
or suffering? I don't know, but I suspect that the answer to all of
those questions is yes. I believe the soul participates in all of our
experiences, but that it is not limited by them. Or maybe what
looks like limitation, depression, or pain on one level can also
look like ascent or spiritual mountain climbing on another.

It's important to consider that point, because spiritual people often have negative attitudes about depression. They might
believe, for instance, that truly spiritual people do not become
depressed, or that depression is a sin, or that it is the result of sin
and guilt, or bad karma, and so on. They might think depression
can never be used by God as a means for personal growth.[1]

Spiritual people do become depressed, though. The story of
Job is a paradigmatic example of this. Job was a man described
as "perfect and upright," who was tested by God, experiencing
terrible losses and becoming depressed. Indeed, one of the reasons he became depressed was *because* he was deeply religious—

and he despaired to think that the God he loved could be so unjust. The kind of despair Job felt is common among spiritual people when they become depressed. If things go badly for them, they see it as evidence that God (or the universe) lacks any justice or goodness.

Yet out of the storm wind of Job's suffering came the voice of God, and transcendental wisdom. At the end of the story, almost as an afterthought, Job was greatly blessed. His depression had been a transformative process, an integral part of his spiritual journey.

But exactly what reply was Job given? What was the answer that illuminated all his darkness and despair? If you read the text of the reply, you'll find it remarkably obscure, leaving itself open to many different interpretations. Perhaps this is a good thing, since it allows the reader to find his or her own answer within it. But it does not even touch on the questions that Job raised: whether suffering means anything, whether justice exists in the world, and so on.

Instead, the reply contains a discussion of how unfathomable and awesome the natural world is:

And YHVH answered Job out of the storm wind, and said . . . By what way is the wind parted, or the east wind scattered upon the earth? . . . Who has divided a watercourse for the torrent of rain, or a way for the thunderous lightning? . . . Who can number the clouds? . . . Who provides for the raven his nourishment? . . . (Job 38)

There are no answers about reality given. There are only deeper and deeper questions, leading us beyond the bounds of our minds. Nature's mysteries, the text seems to say, are themselves echoes of the sacred Mysterious One, pointing to the *Who* behind all things. The very mysteriousness of the universe is the calling card of the Divine. The questions that perplex us and affect us the most—perhaps even triggering a depressed response in us—are really God's address to us, calling us to a deeper awareness.

Martin Buber, the Jewish philosopher and theologian, wrote: "The true answer that Job receives is God's appearance only. . . . Nothing has happened but that man again hears God's address."[2]

And so the reply Job was given was not really an answer; it was only the opening of his eyes and ears to the presence of the Divine Mystery in which he was immersed.

The Darkness That Covers God

A cloud and thick darkness surround [God]. . . .
—PSALM 97

God has made my heart faint . . . because the darkness
was not held back before me, nor did he cover the thick
darkness from before my face.—JOB 23:16–17

The darkness and suffering Job experienced made him feel distant from the Divine, but as he later discovered, that was an illusion—he was actually closer than ever. Medieval Christian mystic Meister Eckhart explained: "Truly, it is in the darkness that one finds the light, so when we are in sorrow, then this light is nearest of all to us."

There is deep wisdom in this. But when we're depressed and we read other people's optimistic words, it often does little more than grate on our nerves. When we are low, the illusions of darkness and distance seem real to us, as they did to Job. It is as though the Divine is covered with a veil that hides its form from us. Its true form beneath the veil we believe to be loving-kindness, and in our everyday life, we can vaguely see the outlines of this. As we come closer to the Divine, though, and closer to the veil that covers it, we lose sight of its overall form, and all we can see is the close-up fabric of the veil; all we can see is the darkness that covers God.

Can we see beyond the veil? We need to temporarily give up our normal ways of seeing for a new way. We need to see with the eyes of the soul.

The Soul's Vision

I had heard of you by the hearing of the ear,
but now my eye sees You.—JOB 42:5

Job's vision of the Divine was utterly transforming for him. How did he attain to this? Only by earnestly questing and questioning, and by refusing to delude himself with the easy answers of the pious, self-righteous men who came to "comfort" him. Only his own personal encounter with the Divine Mystery had any meaning to him.

We, too, need to find our own visions. We are each unique beings, and so while the words of others can help us, we need to find our own understanding, one that no one has ever discovered before. Your soul already has this vision. You only need to learn to see with it.

Around the year 1910, an Arapaho man gave the following account to an ethnographer. In this dream healing, the man was given his soul's vision: a beautiful and spiritually empowering new perspective on the world. Read it slowly and feel its strength; it is hair-raising.

> *He saw himself standing alone on a green prairie, looking to the east. On his left, to the north, he then saw a person seated, dressed entirely in black silk. He thought that this was the messenger. The man wanted to approach him and touch him; but his thoughts were not strong enough, and he was unable to move. Then this person in black spoke to him. He knew all the man's thoughts. He told him of the new world that was to be, and that they were now on a cloud. Then [the man] . . . saw*

*the earth below him and the sky above him. The person in
black, who was the crow, then showed him a rainbow extend-
ing from east to west, and another from north to south. . . .
[The man] was then taken by him to the spot where the two
rainbows crossed one another. There he stood, and the crow
told him to look up. He then saw where the father was, and
saw the thoughts of all mankind reaching up to him [the
father]. . . .* [3]

You will know if your dream is a true vision because it will be
clear and lucid; it might seem more real than everyday waking
reality. Even more important, your soul's true vision will
empower you with respect and empathy for others, and give you
hope and a new depth to your life. If it does not do these things,
you will know that it is not your soul's vision, but that it came
from a shallower, less real level.

To attune yourself to be able to see with your soul's true
vision, you need to consciously respect your own spirituality
and, preferably, immerse yourself in it. This will prepare you for
the deepest level of healing.

Is Spirituality the Ultimate Therapy?

*Help us to be the always-hopeful gardeners of the spirit
who know that without darkness nothing comes to birth,
as without light nothing flowers.*—MAY SARTON

Healing is becoming aware of what we are here for.
—ANONYMOUS

Before going any further, there is an important question to ask.
If the depressed response, or even major depressive disorder, is
part of your spiritual journey, will involving yourself in more
spiritual activities resolve or cure it? Is spirituality the ultimate
therapy?

I think it can be, but it is not necessarily so for everybody at all times. What we call "spiritual" activities—prayer, meditation, and healing by the laying on of hands—have a very real power to heal. There are an impressive and growing number of controlled scientific studies that have demonstrated this. Spiritual healing, for example, has been shown to significantly lower blood pressure, relieve asthma attacks, speed wound healing, decrease anxiety and pain, and to help many other conditions.[4] Intensive involvement in spiritual activities is also seen by shamans as crucial for obtaining healing medicine dreams.

On the other hand, I think we all go through cycles of spiritual need. At various times in our lives, we very much feel the need to be spiritually oriented. It is right for us to do so then. At other times, we feel the need to focus on other aspects of our lives, and it is the right thing to do then, too. It is not so much that those other times are unspiritual, it is more that they are times when our spirituality is expressed differently. We might be focusing more on raising our children or on earning a living than on attending religious services or meditating twice a day.

Ideally, spirituality is about how we relate to all people and all things in the world. It can't be compartmentalized. Everything we do in our lives is part of our soul's journey. So if now is a time when it doesn't feel right for you to be consciously spiritual, that's fine. But if the time is right, follow your spirit.

Meditation

Learn to get in touch with the silence within yourself and know that everything in this life has a purpose.
—ELISABETH KÜBLER-ROSS

[T]he very identity of the Soul with the Beloved, of G-d with the Person, is already a fact. . . . Periodic reflection on this truth is spiritual medicine for depression at any stage of practice.—RABBI ZALMAN SCHACHTER-SHALOMI

Meditation is a natural healing source. Recent studies have shown that if practiced regularly, it has a real power to improve feelings of anxiety, depression, and hostility.[5] When you are in the midst of a depressed response, you are already in a state conducive to meditation. It can occur spontaneously, without any technique or preparation. Just as the depressed response activates intense dreaming, it also encourages inwardness and soul-searching meditation. It brings out your spiritual capacities.

Please note, however, that I do not generally recommend meditation for people who have major depressive disorder. In those cases, it may be difficult or impossible to focus the mind adequately, and this can lead to further distress. Meditation, however, may be suitable for some with very mild cases of major depressive disorder. It's also now being used for people who've recovered from severe depression, to prevent relapses.[6]

Even though meditation can occur spontaneously during the depressed response, it can be helpful to have a technique or ritual to act as an introduction. You can also use specific techniques to guide the meditation in the direction you wish. People often develop their own style of meditation after they become familiar with the basic techniques.

All religions have some form of meditation as part of their path, though these practices are often not well known—even among their own members. I encourage you to seek out the varieties of meditation that are part of your belief system or religion.

Meditation does not have to have a formal structure. Sometimes the most profound experiences can be found in seemingly mundane contexts, like watering the lawn. Most people engage in some form of meditation without actually labeling it "meditation" or going out of their way to do it.

I'll present here three different types of meditation. They are very basic and nonreligious in nature, so hopefully they'll be acceptable to people of all beliefs. We'll begin with a meditation on breath.

Meditation on Breath

Our breath—always with us—is a safe, gentle thing to start with. At the same time, it is an unparalleled gateway to the unconscious, and to the superconscious. Because breathing is an unconscious process that can also be controlled by the conscious mind, it is a bridge between these two realms of awareness. Most spiritual traditions also see breathing as a link with the superconscious, or divine realm; our soul is said to have been "breathed" into us, for example.

The object of this meditation is to be able to focus your mind entirely on your breath, not allowing extraneous thoughts to disturb that focus. (If you are not comfortable with focusing on your breath, you can focus on something else. You might try a flower, a candle flame, a word [like "One"], or your heartbeat.)

Preparation for your meditation can be of help. Take a shower, or wash your hands and face, and put on clean, loose clothing. Music for meditation or incense is helpful for some people but distracting for others. Set aside ten minutes for yourself, and go to a quiet room where you will not be interrupted. You might want to set a timer if you're concerned about losing track of time. Sit down comfortably, in a position that takes minimal effort to maintain. Now take three slow, deep breaths, focusing on the movement of your abdomen and then your chest; filling and emptying your lungs with each breath.

Concentrate now on breathing slowly and steadily through your nose, filling and emptying your lungs with each breath, keeping your mouth closed. Imagine that there is a thread hanging from the tip of your nose, right between your nostrils, and breathe slowly and steadily enough so that the thread does not move to either side.

This can be difficult at first, and you might have to stop a few times to breathe normally. That's okay—just keep going back to focusing on your breath and the thread.

If other thoughts intrude, let them alone, and continue to focus on your breathing. Efforts to push other thoughts away will only end up strengthening them; they will go away on their own if you continue to focus on your breathing.

This is not a competition, so don't worry about evaluating your skill. Have compassion on yourself.

Keep at this for five to ten minutes. Then, take three big breaths as you did at the beginning, and just sit quietly for a minute or two. If you like, you can do this twice a day, but once a day is fine. You are learning the basics, there's no need to rush. If you find you are too keyed up to concentrate, you could try a relaxation exercise instead (see Chapter 17).

If you are using this meditation as a regular exercise when you're feeling well, gradually increase its length as you become more comfortable with it. During the second and third weeks, extend your period of meditation to fifteen minutes, using a timer. Even if you're having difficulty with concentrating for the whole fifteen minutes, keep at it. With practice, your ability to focus will improve, placing you in touch with the power of the quiet mind.

This meditation on breath is excellent on its own, but it is also a useful preparation for other types of meditation. After you've reached a degree of familiarity with quieting the mind through breathing exercises, you can use this quieted state for the contemplation of other things.

Meditation on Infinity

You might try the following exercise involving the contemplation of the concept of infinity. In a rational, linear way of thinking, infinity can only be considered as an abstract idea. It is impossible to give it size or shape. The intuitive, nonlinear mind, however, is not subject to this restriction, and is able to consider infinity in a more direct manner.

After quieting your mind using the meditation on breath, keep your eyes closed. Then begin by visualizing the space around you in the room. Expand your visualized space in all directions to include the building, then the whole block, then the suburb, town, or city. Continue on to the county, state, and nation; continent, planet, solar system, galaxy, galactic cluster, on to the farthest objects in space, and continue outward. Eventually you will come to the limit of the range of the linear mind, and it will want to give up. Keep pressing on toward infinity regardless. The nonlinear mind must take over.

When you get even a vague, fleeting glimpse of what the concept of infinity means, you can experience an intense feeling of compassion for all things subject to limitations, including yourself. The next time you find yourself in a difficult circumstance, recall that feeling and let it help guide your actions.

Meditation on Being Present

A lot of pain and stress occurs over worries about the future and regrets about the past. Caught up in these concerns, we lose sight of where we really are—in the present. By concentrating entirely on what you are doing now, paying close attention to all the sensations available to you, it's sometimes like your eyes have just been opened to the world. This is a meditation you can do at any time, without any special preparation. It's easiest, though, if you're doing something that doesn't require a lot of concentration, like eating or walking.

Using walking as an example, a meditation on being present goes something like this: On your walk, allow your attention to be focused, one by one, on the variety of simple sensations you are experiencing. Look around yourself and notice the position of everything around you. Feel the movement of air on your face, and the heat of the sun. Feel the presence of the clothing on your skin, and the movement of your limbs as you walk, and the sensations arising in them. Feel your feet contact the ground, and gravity holding you there. Hear the sounds around you—of traffic, or birds, or other things. Are there any scents you can detect? And so on.

Sometimes, when you do this, your mind will say, "Hey! You can't focus on all those things right now—what about all these problems that need solving?" Tell yourself that it's okay to focus on the present just for a little while, and that you'll get back to the problems later. When you do get back to them, you'll have a new energy and efficiency. Being really present in the moment for even a brief time is very refreshing.

A Way of Anchoring Yourself

Throughout the day, whenever possible, and especially in stressful situations, try applying the same techniques of focusing on your breath or of focusing on the sensations of the present. If you are feeling carried away in a stream of stress, worries, or other negative states, this heightened awareness of the here and now will act like an anchor for you.

Prayer

From the depths I have called to You . . .—PSALM 130

Prayer is not really in the same category as meditation. While it is also an intensely personal thing, prayer looks outward, rather than inward toward one's experiences.

Most people have prayed spontaneously at some point in their lives—it is a natural, human response when confronting a crisis. It has real power, and should not be underestimated.

When you are depressed, your prayers have a special significance. According to the Jewish and Christian traditions, God listens more closely to the prayers of the brokenhearted and the sick than to any others. So it is a time to immerse yourself in prayer, and to pray that your soul's vision be granted.

Prayer can be comforting, but not in every case. Sometimes no amount of praying seems to make any difference. Sometimes the absence of a reply means solace cannot be had. If prayer is really about speaking to an Other—a Self beyond one's own self—then perhaps the reply can come in a form we do not expect, or at a time when we do not expect it. Or the reply might not come in the form of a solution to a problem, but in the form of you being granted access to a deeper level of understanding about the problem or about yourself.

Prayer is really about more than just expecting a reply. It is a way of affirming that we are not alone in the world.

How does one pray? Every spiritual tradition contains a variety of ways to pray. One technique is to find a written prayer you like or to make one up. Then, as you are saying the words, enter into them; try to feel all their meanings and nuances. If you can't contact the feelings evoked by the words, try to visualize the letters of the words filling your inner being. In this way, instead of merely saying the prayer, you *become* the prayer in the inner world.

Religion

Religion—that voice of deepest human experience.
—MATTHEW ARNOLD

What about involvement in established religion—is that a good idea for people who are depressed?

Many psychiatrists and psychologists will tell you that it isn't. This, however, has more to do with their own prejudices than anything else. In fact, the research data shows that involvement in religious activity is strongly protective for mental health.[7]

Historically, the scientific professions have viewed religion in terms of pathology. This point of view dates from the age of the Enlightenment, a philosophical movement in the eighteenth century whose goal was to free rationality and morality from what was seen as the superstitiousness of religion. Taken in those terms, we're still living in the age of Enlightenment.

Sigmund Freud's view, for example, was that religion represented a type of "universal obsessional neurosis," and this view continues to be widely held.[8] It's interesting to note that over 50 percent of psychiatrists and psychologists are self-declared atheists, in contrast to the figure for the general population, which is 1 to 5 percent.[9]

In spite of this, quite a large number of studies have been nearly unanimous in showing that religious belief or involvement is a strongly protective factor in mental and physical health. For example, it is protective for depression, suicide, substance abuse, delinquency, physical ill-health in general, and so on.[10] This is not to say that religious people do not become depressed, it is just less common among them.

You could speculate at length on the reasons for this protective effect, but one of the most important ones is probably that religion provides many age-old mechanisms for coping with stressors. Some have even claimed that this is the main function of religion. I think that human beings are intrinsically spiritual creatures, and that at times we can greatly benefit from the framework of spiritual life that organized religion offers.

On the other hand, many valid criticisms of organized religion can be made. Its ways of seeing the world are often rigidly defined, and individuality of thought and action is not encouraged. This can stifle a person's development. Religious involvement, though protective for depression, also predisposes to overcontrol and perfectionism as personality traits.[11]

In summary, religion can have much to offer you, but you need to approach it in a balanced way, and with moderation. Finding a harmonious blend between preserving your individuality and adopting the ways of religion is the key. This can enable you to maintain and deepen your qualities of spirituality and creativity at the same time. In the next chapter, we'll see that these two qualities go together, and are both essential parts of the soul's journey.

Recommended Reading

Healing Words: The Power of Prayer and the Practice of Medicine by Larry Dossey (San Francisco: Harper, 1993) contains case studies and a discussion of the phenomenon of spiritual healing, and prayer in particular. It also summarizes research in the field, providing scientific support for the reality of spiritual healing.

CHAPTER 4

✦

ENTERING THE HEART
OF CREATIVITY

*Be brave enough to live creatively. The creative is the
place where no one else has ever been. . . . You can't get
there by bus, only by hard work, risking, and by not quite
knowing what you're doing. What you'll discover will be
wonderful: yourself.*—ALAN ALDA

Life Is the Real Art

This above all: to thine own self be true.
—WILLIAM SHAKESPEARE

THERE is a way to make your life work. No matter what circumstances you're facing, you can find a path that will help
you grow, and ultimately enhance your life's journey in ways you
may never have thought of.

How do you get there? More often than not we don't even
know where "there" is. Sometimes even after we've received
our soul's vision, we have no idea how to make it work in our
lives. To find your way when the road isn't clear, you need to
use an important capacity that we all have but often neglect:
creativity.

Thinking creatively is something everyone is capable of
doing quite naturally. It comes part and parcel with the ability to
imagine, to play, and to dream. As children, we spend much of
our time luxuriating in our creativity—remember how we imag-

ined that an old cardboard box was a magic castle or a pirate ship? Creativity is one of the basic modes of operation of our minds. It is a mode that the depressed response encourages in us, to help us find a new way of being in the world.

Then how is it that so many people get locked into a very limited, unimaginative mind-set—doing work they hate, feeling trapped in an unhappy life, and feeling powerless to change things?

The main way creativity is stifled, I think, is by not listening to what your soul is trying to tell you. Your soul doesn't just speak to you in visions. That may be when you can hear it the most clearly, but actually, your soul is always trying to teach you, no matter what you're doing. Everything that happens to us in life is a lesson, constantly creating new levels of understanding within us. If we don't listen to our soul's teachings, we end up stuck in our limitations until we finally learn the lessons they were trying to teach. Only then can we move on creatively to new things. How do you listen? Maybe the best way is to make sure you are doing what you really believe in. Integrity is like a radio receiver that picks up your soul's voice.

Another way that your creativity can be limited is by allowing your life to be run solely according to the expectations of others. By "others" I mean not just parents, relatives, teachers, and friends but also society in general. We unthinkingly take on many of our beliefs, attitudes, and goals from these sources, and this can severely restrict our paths in life. For instance, if we unthinkingly follow the lead of our materialistic, consumer-oriented society, we can end up trapped in an unhappy job to meet the financial demands of all the so-called essential things that are really just luxuries—like another car, cable TV, and so on.

On the one hand, it is healthy up to a point to allow yourself to be influenced by other people's advice. An inability to take advice is a serious handicap. On the other hand, though, you have to be capable of some individuality in your decision-making. What you need, as in all things, is to find the right balance—in this case between catering to other people's wants and needs and your own.

Our educational institutions also stifle our creativity. When education becomes synonymous with the mere memorization of endless facts, and with conforming to things like dress codes and timetables, there's clearly little encouragement to be creative. Instead, our creativity is channeled into enclosed areas like "the Arts." We forget that life itself is the real art; the art that all the other "Arts" are only attempts to imitate. We end up out of practice with ways of using creativity more broadly in our lives.

Rediscovering the Heart of Creativity

How can we start to think creatively again? Once we are in a moment of creativity, it seems to come to us fluidly, without any special effort. It's certainly not the sort of thing that requires step-by-step instructions. But here's the paradox: If you're feeling out of touch with your creativity, you may need to take a few deliberate, seemingly uncreative steps to get back into it.

Here's step one: Take all of this as unseriously as you possibly can. And start playing.

Play—A Wellspring of Life Energy

When you're depressed, your whole body is depressed, and
it translates to the cellular level. The first objective is to
get your energy level up, and you can do it through play.
It's one of the most powerful ways of breaking up hope-
lessness and bringing in energy to the situation.
—DR. O. CARL SIMONTON

What we play is life.—LOUIS ARMSTRONG

Play is a basic human need. It puts us in touch with the wellspring of creative life energy that is in our spirit. The things that you enjoy doing are those that help you express some aspect of yourself in a creative way. They are not just optional amusements in your life; they are *essential* for your well-being.

You may feel you've forgotten how to play. A lot of the time, as we grow up, we let our imaginations atrophy, or we let television and movies supply the flights of imagination that we used to create for ourselves.

Playing involves doing something that has no object other than its innocent enjoyment. If you're depressed, there may not be anything that you can think of that you enjoy doing now. Then again, this might not be because you're depressed, but rather it may be the *reason* you're depressed. Some people systematically exclude from their lives the things they enjoy doing, and this leaves them with little outlet for self-expression. They might have various seemingly "sensible" reasons for doing this, such as being too busy, under pressure, too old, and so on; some have a subconscious desire to punish themselves. But they are pushing themselves off-balance, and there is nothing sensible about that. All work and no play makes you depressed.

Serious Fun

The deeper that sorrow carves into your being, the more
joy you can contain. Is not the cup that holds your wine
the very cup that was burned in the potter's oven?
—KAHLIL GIBRAN

Depression can result from being excessively stern and serious with yourself. How can you bring yourself back into balance? There is an old Hasidic proverb: "The way to straighten a bent sapling is to bend it in the opposite direction." Sometimes, you need to be frivolous to balance yourself out.

If you can't think of anything you enjoy now, think back to the past. Make a list of five things that you once enjoyed doing.

It might be miniature golf. It might be playing fetch with the dog. It might be shooting hoops down at the basketball court. It might be watching a stream flow.

Check out your local community center for classes or sports groups, like a beginning dance class, drama class, or sculpture class. Go to the science or natural history museum and look at the bug collection. Some people's idea of fun might be riding the roller coaster at an amusement park. Another's might be riding the rocking chair on the porch in the evening.

It's important here to make a distinction between creative and destructive enjoyment. Unfortunately, in our society there's a general belief that "fun" for adults means destructive enjoyment, like alcohol abuse, illicit sex, and so on. That we find enjoyment in damaging ourselves and others is really a measure of our alienation from ourselves. But creative enjoyment derives from a deeper level of our being, and it is truer to ourselves.

Art and Creativity

An artist is a dreamer consenting to dream of the actual world.—GEORGE SANTAYANA

It is as a way of increasing your creative abilities that the Arts as therapy really comes into its own. Formalized expressions of creativity can help you develop your ability to respond in an original and fresh way to the rest of your life. I especially mean here the art forms in which you participate, rather than just being a spectator: like painting, writing, dancing, and music.

Art therapy has even been shown scientifically to benefit depressed people.[1] I've found that even the most severely depressed people can derive satisfaction, if not actual enjoyment, from putting their feelings down on paper in an abstract form. It provides them with a way of bringing to consciousness aspects of their situation that may have been previously suppressed. It enables them to externalize their problems and perhaps see them more objectively. Often it's used as a way to communicate feelings that are difficult or impossible to express verbally. I've found that a person's artwork provides an excellent focal point for a therapy session.

One patient, for example, brought to my office a series of crayon sketches. One of them was of her house. In the window, she had drawn an image of herself. As she showed it to me, she realized that her husband was not in the picture. This realization was meaningful to her, she said, since she felt it expressed her fear that her husband would leave her because of her illness. In this way, a previously subconscious issue was brought to light and she was then able to discuss it. And incidentally, her husband did not leave her.

Even if you don't share your artwork with your therapist, I recommend you do some art therapy on your own. Purchase a box of crayons and some drawing paper and/or some watercolors, colored pencils, whatever. Draw and paint your feelings or scenes from your dreams.

Some people have inhibitions about drawing and painting, because they think they won't be "good enough" at it. But it doesn't have to be of museum quality. In fact, I say the messier the work, the more therapeutic it is for some people. Sometimes what people really need is just to make a mess for once, as a way to start getting over the perfectionism and overcontrol that limits them.

Your artwork doesn't have to provide you with any great psychotherapeutic breakthroughs, either. It's worth doing just for fun.

Music and Dance

O Music! . . . Friend of Pleasure, Wisdom's aid!
—WILLIAM COLLINS, c. 1750

It's official: Music lifts depression. Many studies have shown that music has a marked effect on mood and self-esteem.[2]

Music is a direct route to the emotional realm. It can be relaxing and healing, or it can be jarring and upsetting. For example, one study found that Vienna waltzes and Mozart's piano concertos improved depression, but other types of music worsened it.[3] Loud or harsh music, or songs with sad lyrics, have a negative effect, but gentle, melodic music and songs with upbeat lyrics have a positive effect.[4] None of this is really a surprise to anybody.

These days, you will find many excellent tapes and CD's of music specifically designed for relaxation, meditation, and healing. They actually work; so give them a try.

Most powerful of all is when music is combined with dance. Dance is about being present in your body in a way people rarely are. Joy is built into dancing and can come from learning new step sequences, moving to a rhythm, experiencing a sense of balance or fluidity when other people are doing the same steps, or in just expressing yourself.

The Path of Words

Said my Muse to me, "Look into thy heart and write."
—SIR PHILIP SYDNEY, c. 1570

Free intuitive writing is a therapeutic technique that could help you solve your deepest problems. It is a way of allowing your subconscious thoughts to surface and be given expression. It can help you understand your thought processes and the effects they have on you.[5]

We are taught in school how to make our writing conform to established forms: grammar, sentence structure, story construction, and so on. This can limit our ability to express our thoughts, especially the amorphous, unstructured thoughts of the subconscious. In free intuitive writing, you allow yourself to follow any path or stream of consciousness that you come across. You allow yourself to be involved entirely in the process of writing rather than worrying about what the finished product will be like. This frees up your creativity from the constraints of the standard forms.

Dialogue writing is another form of therapeutic prose. It involves the creation of an imaginary discussion between yourself and another person, thing, or event. It might be a discussion between you and an aspect of your personality, a feeling, your future or past self, an imaginary or real person, or other such things. For example, if you are sick you could ask a part of your body why it is hurting so much, and what message it is trying to give you. These dialogues can be very healing.

Here is an example of what a dialogue might be like; this one is between a person and an aspect of her personality that is named Critic:

SELF: Critic, why were you so mean to me today?

CRITIC: You were doing everything wrong.

SELF: But calling me names like "Stupid" and "Idiot" really hurt. Was I really doing *everything* wrong?

CRITIC: Okay, you were doing *some* things wrong, not everything. I was punishing you because I just wanted to make sure you wouldn't make those mistakes again. I was trying to protect you from your mistakes.

SELF: I appreciate your trying to help, but hurting my feelings isn't helping. Can you try a different way of protecting me?

CRITIC: I don't know any other way.

SELF: Maybe you could focus on telling me what I did *right* instead of what I did wrong. I'd feel a lot more encouraged.

CRITIC: Well . . . I'll give it a try for a while, and see how it goes.

SELF: Okay, and thanks. We ought to have chats more often.

Writing can also be a way for you to avoid excessive worrying—dedicating a brief time to putting your worries down on paper means you can allow yourself to focus on other things later. I also encourage you to record your dreams in a journal set aside for this purpose.

Expressing creativity is important for everybody, not just people with depression. It is more than just a healing activity, it is a way of living fully. Through play, art, music, dance, writing, and other such activities, you can increase your creative abilities in a way that can be carried over into the whole of your life. In the next chapter, we'll look at ways of applying your creativity to problems you are facing.

CHAPTER 5

✦

CREATIVE SOLUTIONS

The key to survival is to embrace the transition, not to
resist it. People should participate in the transition,
creatively, like they really want it.
—*MAD BEAR, NATIVE AMERICAN SHAMAN*

TRANSFORMATION is not just an inner task. It needs to occur
outwardly as well, so that you can fully resolve the problem
that led to you developing your depressed response. That's why
being totally inwardly focused during the depressed response can
sometimes not be enough. Sometimes the resolution will only
come when you involve yourself with the outer aspects of the
problem, by going out into the world and working for a solution,
or by going to other people for advice.

If your depressed response has been going on for a while, say
for five days or so, and it is going nowhere—not really helping
you—it's time for you to become outwardly focused. Inner creativity, as described in the last chapter, is still an essential part of
the healing process. But your outward actions can actually boost
your overall creativity.

New York psychiatrist Dr. Frederic Flach believes that the
process of creative problem solving can be enhanced through
practice. In his book *Resilience—Discovering a New Strength at*
Times of Stress, he writes that the process takes place in five
stages.[1] Some stages can occur virtually instantaneously; others
can require prolonged "simmering." They can occur both
inwardly, through flashes of inspiration or intuition, or outwardly, by taking a series of deliberate steps, as I'll discuss.

Gathering Information

Knowledge is power.—FRANCIS BACON

The first stage of creative problem solving, Dr. Flach writes, is to collect as much information about the situation as possible. This means seeking the opinions of other people involved in the situation, reading widely around the topic, and perhaps consulting with experts. I agree with Dr. Flach on the importance of this stage. I've often been impressed, for instance, at how much better patients do when they make the effort to learn all they can about their illness, and to become creatively involved in their therapy. This principle would also apply to other sorts of difficulties you might be facing in life, whether they involve finances, employment, relationships, or simpler things.

Redefining the Problem

There's no such thing as doomsday—only the end of one era and the beginning of another.
—MAD BEAR, NATIVE AMERICAN SHAMAN

The second stage of the process involves the redefinition of the problem—seeing it in a new light. The way we define things sometimes places restrictions on what we feel we can do about them. Redefining the situation can give you new insights and a fresh approach. For example, Dr. Flach suggests that a problem in a marriage could be redefined from "Why are we always fighting?" to "How could we get along better?" Likewise, problems with a job might be redefined from "My long working hours mean I don't have enough time for my family" to "Why am I working so hard? What are my real goals in life? Are there other companies with better working conditions? Should I work in this field at all?"

Redefinition is an important, even essential, part of the transformative healing process, whether it involves redefinition of your problems or of the characteristics of your inner self. Redefinition can happen logically, by carefully viewing the situation from many different angles and trying to be objective and fair about it. Or it can happen intuitively, through flashes of inspiration that grant you access to deeper levels of understanding. Medicine dreams can serve this purpose for you. By consciously collecting all the information you can, you will provide your subconscious mind with the raw material it needs to form its intuitive response. This response can be made accessible to your conscious mind through your dreams and their symbols.

If you are unable to redefine the problem on your own, discuss it with a therapist—an objective viewpoint can be very useful. Redefinition is actually one of the basic healing modalities used in psychotherapy.

Finding Options

The dogmas of the quiet past are inadequate to the stormy present. . . . As our case is new, so we must think anew and act anew.—ABRAHAM LINCOLN, 1862

The third stage consists of finding all your options for dealing with the newly redefined problem. For example, now that the couple have redefined the problem to be "How can we get along better?" they could explore ways in which they could show more thoughtfulness and respect to each other, and discuss activities that they could share. The person whose job was taking too much time away from his family life could, for instance, speak to his supervisor about decreasing his workload. He could explore his options for alternative employment by speaking to job-placement experts, career counselors, or personnel directors in other companies. Taking a job closer to home, for example, would cut down on his commuting time and give him more time at home.

The more options you can find, the better: Quantity here leads to quality. Don't be quick to dismiss any option; give them all a fair assessment.

Choosing a Path

Two roads diverged in a wood, and I—
I took the one less traveled by,
And that has made all the difference.
—ROBERT FROST

In the fourth stage, you weigh the pros and cons of your various options and contrast them with your needs. The person with the employment problem might be unable to get by with less pay. This might rule out the option of a reduced workload and instead mean he'd have to take the option of changing companies, or careers. In other words, in this stage you attempt to make as realistic and rational a choice as possible.

Transmuting Thoughts into Reality

Blessed is he who has found his work.
—THOMAS CARLYLE, c. 1860

You work that you may keep pace with the earth and the
soul of the earth. . . . Work is love made visible.
—KAHLIL GIBRAN

In the final stage, the chosen option is put into action. To do this, you need to make a plan, and have enough self-discipline to carry it through. Patience, too, will probably be required. Don't be afraid of hard work if that's what you need to do. If it is really part of your soul's path, know that you have already been given the strength to do it. The energy for the task is there.

By breaking down the creative problem-solving process into these five stages and working through them one at a time, it becomes much less daunting. When you're facing situations that seem to overwhelm you, it's easier to deal with them in small steps than to tackle them all at once. Do the little things that you can do now, and those small achievements will help give you the confidence to continue on to do the big things. Then finally, you can come to a full resolution of the situation.

The Resilient Bodymind

Numberless are the world's wonders, but none
More wonderful than man.
—SOPHOCLES, c. 420 B.C.E.

In this first part of the book, we've looked at the depressed response. We've explored how it's designed to help you, and how you can cooperate with it consciously to enhance its effectiveness, both inwardly and outwardly. The response is just one of the many remarkable features "built in" to the human bodymind that make us such a resilient and adaptable species.

But what about the minority of cases that don't resolve on their own? In the next part of the book we'll explore the reasons why some people's innate healing abilities become blocked, and why their depressed responses don't achieve their goal of inner and outer transformation. We'll look at the many fascinating ways the body and mind interact, and we'll see that this deep-rooted interaction means that a vulnerability in any part of our being can affect all other parts at once.

✦

PART II

When Depression Becomes an Illness

There is no wisdom in useless and hopeless sorrow.
—*DR. SAMUEL JOHNSON, c. 1750*

✦

CHAPTER 6

THE UNRESOLVED RESPONSE

*There are so many things in human living that we should
regard not as traumatic learning but as incomplete
learning, unfinished learning.*
—*MILTON ERIKSON*

SOMETIMES, when we reach an impasse in life, the depressed
response is a necessity, as I discussed in the previous section.
It can help us to dive deep into ourselves, to restructure our
inner being, and come to a new way of understanding and living
in the world.

So why is it that the depressed response sometimes doesn't
succeed in helping us, and instead turns into an illness? There are
many reasons for this. The response involves all levels of a person's being, so it can potentially be blocked or disrupted on any
level—mental, physical, social, or spiritual. Let's look at some of
the ways this can happen.

Avoided Depression

*Great pain, when it is honored from the heart, opens into
great understanding.*—*JACK KORNFIELD*

Many people have some deep sense of distress in their lives that
they strenuously try to push into their subconscious and ignore.
If the distress is not dealt with consciously, then the process of
depression would be the natural way for it to be resolved.

Our society in general, however, does not understand the healing function of our natural responses, especially the depressed response. We see all feelings of depression as unacceptable or pathological. This means that the normal depressed response is often avoided, or inappropriately suppressed with medication. This in turn means that people do not achieve the development and maturation they require and are left more vulnerable to severe stress, and ever more severe breakdowns.

Some people are reluctant to initiate or resolve their depression because of a lack of confidence in themselves or in the world. They might be afraid that if the process starts, they will be unable to get out of it again. For others, its resolution might be blocked because they feel unable to change. Their fear holds them back. Healing often requires courage and a willingness to take a risk.

To push the depressed response back down into their subconscious, and divert themselves from self-confrontation, many people use addictions—overwork, food obsession, alcoholism, drug abuse, gambling, escapist entertainment. But sooner or later the distress must well up again, and the process cries out to be completed. So addictions and all the misery that goes along with them are often the results of our lack of trust in our natural responses. I think that avoided depression is a major cause of arrested personal development and chronic ill health in our society.

Joseph's Story

"Ten years of heavy drinking, that's what's led me here," said Joseph, sinking his head into his hands, sitting in my office on the psychiatric ward. "But I gave it all up four months ago, and haven't touched alcohol since. . . . I thought I'd gotten all that behind me. Now, in a lot of ways, I'm worse than ever—more depressed. This wasn't supposed to happen. . . ."

Joseph was forty-five years old and had gone back to university to finish his master's in psychology. So when he said he couldn't understand what was happening with his feelings, it wasn't through lack of intelligence or effort. He had analyzed himself more intensely than any therapist could.

"Of course I was never happy when I was drinking, but I could handle it then. I mean, that's why I drank, to handle it. Now . . . I look into my heart, and it's just empty." Over the next few weeks in the hospital, Joseph spent a lot of time crying. He was severely depressed, and required medication and intensive psychotherapy. Gradually, he pieced himself back together, with many peaks and valleys in his progress.

One morning, after about a month in the hospital, he talked about an insight he had come to. He told me that since he had stopped drinking, he felt he had, in effect, taken up where he'd left off years ago in dealing with the traumas and griefs of his unhappy adolescence and young adulthood. He said that his drinking had been a way to avoid dealing with them. Now, though, he wasn't running away from himself anymore. Returning to school, he said, had been an additional, outward manifestation of the process of picking up where he'd left off.

He was at last dealing with his suppressed feelings and could once more see himself growing and evolving. Through this, he started to feel a sense of his own strength. He recovered fully from his depression, and is now in practice himself, with the kind of ability to help others that can only come from personal experience.

Fortunately, not everyone recovering from an addiction becomes depressed—and, certainly, few become as depressed as Joseph had been. But his was a classic example of the way addictions can be an avoidance of the healing and transformative work of depression. His story also shows us that even a severe depression can be turned around.

Unresolved Depression

*We have left undone the things which we ought to have
done. . . . And there is no health in us.*
—BOOK OF COMMON PRAYER, c. 1549

Once the flow of creative energy from the subconscious bodymind has been allowed to initiate the depressed response, the
person remains in an unstable, disoriented, and vulnerable state
until a new inner synthesis is formed. Under favorable conditions, this should not take long. If a psychological or physical
problem blocks the depressed response, however, there is a risk
that its resolution may only be partial. The person may get stuck
in a holding pattern, circling around in a state of continuing dis-
ability and limitation.

There may be factors in the environment, for instance, that
make any sort of meaningful change very difficult. The person
might have grown up in a family where people's roles were very
rigidly defined, and where no possibility of change could be considered for fear of upsetting the status quo. Or the person might
be living in an abusive relationship, and not feel she has the emotional space or safety to express herself or to grow.

Physical problems can also disrupt the process. Some people
have a genetic predisposition toward poor resolution of the
depressed response. Once the response has started, their body-
minds seem unable to resolve it without help. Many physical illnesses can also unbalance the physical pathways in the brain and
body that are involved in producing the depressed response, as
I'll discuss in the next chapter.

If the impediments are serious enough, the depressed
response may not be resolvable at all. In that case, it would
become unproductive, chronic, and self-perpetuating. It would
then no longer be an adaptive response but an illness. Judy's
story shows us how this can happen.

Judy's Story

Somewhere along the line, Judy's depressed response had gotten stuck. Now in her mid-forties, she had been in an almost continuous state of depression for over fifteen years. In this time, she'd had eight admissions to psychiatric hospitals. Clearly, the treatment she'd received had not gotten to the root of the problem. But what were the factors that were preventing her from recovering?

Her brother was mildly brain damaged from an accident, and since they were both estranged from their parents, the task of looking after him had fallen to her. Unfortunately, he was very difficult to get along with. She spent much of her time either fighting with him, doing his housework, or worrying about him. Free time was hard to find, but then, she had no outside interests or friends anyway. Her world was an enclosed, unending struggle.

It was obvious that her situation at home was the major factor in maintaining her illness. She needed more help in looking after her brother, which would give her the chance to spend time outside the home. She needed to start doing something productive for herself for a change.

I contacted a day-care center for people with intellectual disabilities, and after going through a lot of red tape, managed to get them to accept her brother—no small feat in these days of underfunded public services. Now that she would have her weekdays free, I encouraged her to continue her education. At first she was shocked that a doctor could recommend something like that, instead of just prescribing more drugs as she'd become accustomed to. After considering the idea for a week or so, though, she summoned up the courage to enroll in a program for training art therapists. She also used nutritional and exercise therapies to round out her holistic treatment plan (see Part III for information on these).

Once she started the course, a huge change came over her. She began to feel that she could be an effective person after all. By breaking the cycle of the denial of her own needs, a new sense of self-esteem was born. Her mood, her energy, and, remarkably, even her posture improved. Her brother started to respect her more, too.

It is almost two years since she began her studies. She's looking forward to graduating, and to her first paid job. She has not had another relapse of depression.

Judy's story is a good example of the way restrictive life circumstances can block the resolution of the depressed response. Her story also demonstrates how a change can free up the way to recovery, even when the response has turned into a chronic illness.

When Depression Becomes an Illness

When a person's depression reaches a certain degree of severity, psychiatrists use the term *major depressive disorder* to describe it. I feel the name is appropriate, since rather than just being "depression," which, as I've said, can be an adaptive response, it describes a state of seriously "disordered depression."

With every type of healing response, there is some degree of risk that it will become disordered, and no longer be adaptive for the individual. For example, if a person accidentally ate a toxic substance, and then produced such an uncontrolled vomiting response that they died from dehydration, that would clearly be maladaptive. Because the response had failed to limit itself normally, it would need to be treated as a disorder in its own right. If the vomiting was very severe and did not respond to supportive therapy like intravenous rehydration, it would need to be suppressed with medication to save the person's life.

In a similar manner, a depressed response that has escalated to the point of becoming an illness needs to be treated. In many cases, conventional medications should be used. These drugs basically interrupt the process of depression. Although the depressed response is natural and healthy, and should be allowed to resolve itself, major depressive disorder is another story altogether. It isn't healthy, and it doesn't reflect the ideal of nature; it definitely *should* be interrupted.

Do you have major depressive disorder? A summary of its strict definition can be found in the table below. In real life, things come in shades and degrees, so some flexibility with the criteria is allowed. Many people with the illness may not necessarily meet all the classic criteria. It's important for you to respect your own feelings about how you're doing, as well as to gain feedback from an outside source.

Criteria for Major Depressive Disorder[1]

These criteria include five or more of the following symptoms over a two-week period, occurring daily or nearly every day, and one of the symptoms must be either (1) depressed mood most of the day, or (2) loss of interest or pleasure in life:

1. depressed mood most of the day
2. loss of interest or pleasure in life
3. change in appetite, or weight loss of more than 5 percent of body weight
4. insomnia or excessive sleep
5. acting or feeling agitated, or slowed down
6. fatigue or loss of energy
7. feelings of worthlessness or excessive, inappropriate guilt
8. poor concentration or indecisiveness
9. recurrent thoughts of death or suicide, or a suicide plan or attempt

Major depressive disorder is one of the most common of all illnesses. About 15 percent of people experience it at some time in their lives. Some studies show that up to 25 percent of women have gone through it.[2]

Why are women more likely than men to become depressed? Researchers believe that the different social and psychological expectations and pressures that women experience have a lot to do with it. The effects of childbirth and hormonal differences probably also play a role. Some doctors believe, though, that depression is actually just as common in men; it's just that men don't acknowledge their feelings, or they express them differently. Men will more often turn to alcohol or drugs to "medicate" themselves rather than see a doctor.

Major depressive disorder is equally common in all races and social classes, and it can begin at any age. It is more common in people who have no close interpersonal relationships, or who are divorced or separated.[3] Being alone makes us more vulnerable.

The Uniqueness of Experience

This may seem surprising to you, but many people who are depressed do not even know it. The reason for this is because depression can produce a bewildering variety of symptoms. The uniqueness of each person makes their expression of the illness unique, and this can make it hard to recognize. Because I've seen hundreds of patients with depression, I've become aware of just how different the illness can seem in each case.

One middle-aged woman, for example, came to me with symptoms of irritability and anger that she couldn't understand. A teenage boy I saw worried that he had Alzheimer's disease, since he felt he had lost his memory. A middle-aged businessman's main complaint was anxiety. A young woman presented with tiredness and overeating. An elderly man saw life as boring and a waste. Another middle-aged woman came to me with complaints of pain throughout her body. Yet after in-depth evaluations, it was clear that all of these people were suffering from major depressive disorder.

Depression also tends to exaggerate a person's character traits. A person who is a worrier will worry more, an angry person will become angrier, and a poor sleeper will become sleepless. The illness distorts people's personalities, sometimes making them seem a caricature of their true selves. Patients (and their families) have sometimes told me after their recovery that they recognized that their true self was really much different from the person they seemed to be during their illness. This was a great relief to them.

If you have symptoms of depression, it's important that you get professional assistance to meet your needs. No book could ever replace the healing power of a therapeutic relationship. By all means, if you're feeling overwhelmed or suicidal, reach out and get the help you need immediately. Chapter 9 discusses ways of finding the physician or therapist who is right for you.

CHAPTER 7

✦

MIND AND BODY

Here in this body are the sacred rivers: here are the sun
and moon as well as all the pilgrimage places. . . . I
have not encountered another temple as blissful as
my own body.—SARAHA

The body is not only more mysterious than we know, it is
also more mysterious than we can know.
—ANONYMOUS

The Oneness of Mind and Body

EMOTION is a physical thing. Depression happens not only in
your mind but in your body as well, down to your very cells
and the biochemical reactions in them. Recent research has given
us fascinating insights into the ways the mind and body interact,
and how depression and stress are processes that affect us on all
levels of our being at once.

Many of the functions that we commonly believe to be
purely "mental" in fact occur not just in our mind but in our
bodymind. This applies to feelings of depression as well as to
happiness, anxiety, love, anger, wonder, and all the many other
feelings and sensations that we experience. The physical reflections of these psychological states can actually be measured by
blood tests and other types of laboratory investigation.

When we become stressed or depressed, for example, many
specific changes occur in the body. Levels of a number of hormones and neurotransmitters are altered. The functioning of cells

in the immune system and nervous system changes. Resistance to infection is decreased. We feel physical pain more acutely, as our brain produces less of its own natural painkilling chemicals (endorphins). The sleep/wake cycle is upset. There is often a change in bowel habits, usually toward constipation. Food smells and tastes differently. The libido changes, usually diminishing markedly. Even the electrical conductivity of skin is altered.

Interestingly, there are a number of drugs that can produce the same symptoms of depression—physical and emotional— through purely chemical means. There is even a herb that can do this—*Rauwolfia serpentina,* or snakeroot, used in Ayurvedic medicine since ancient times for various nervous disorders. On the other hand, emotional stress alone can also cause all of these symptoms. Clearly, the physical and emotional aspects of our being are deeply intertwined.

In this chapter, I'll show you how the different aspects of your being are integrated into one—how what happens in your mind affects your physical body, and vice versa. As you'll see, all of these aspects need to be considered as we search for the causes of depression.

How Stress Causes Depression

In today's world, we are all prone to becoming stressed-out; so much so that we generally take it for granted. Stress is not just a minor nuisance, though. Severe or chronic stress can damage your bodymind and lead to major depressive disorder. Although the reasons for this are not completely understood, scientists believe that it may have something to do with the way many people seem unable to switch off their stress reactions.

Let's take a look at what happens in your bodymind when you encounter a difficult problem and feel stressed. Your brain sends a chemical message through the bloodstream to your adrenal glands, which are two small triangular glands located next to your kidneys. The message tells your adrenals to increase their production of the hormones epinephrine and cortisol. Both of these hormones are intended to help you deal with whatever is stressing you.

Epinephrine's effects occur rapidly, and are probably familiar to you—a racing heart, increased blood flow to the muscles, and a heightened state of alertness. Cortisol's effects take at least several hours to be produced, and they are less easily felt. Cortisol boosts your blood sugar to provide extra energy, and it also suppresses inflammation. The purpose of these actions is to minimize the fatigue and pain that might otherwise slow you down in a stressful situation. High epinephrine and cortisol levels would give you a distinct advantage, for example, if you were running from a bear, or you were a soldier in hand-to-hand combat.

You don't need to be in a physically threatening situation, however, for the stress response to be triggered. Even situations involving only psychological or mental difficulties can produce the very same response. For example, if you are taking a difficult math test, or being reprimanded by your boss, you will probably have increased levels of epinephrine and cortisol in your bloodstream. In these sorts of situations, these stress hormones can provide you with the extra energy and alertness you need to do well and achieve your best. While these effects are helpful in the short term, your bodymind cannot maintain this stimulated state for long without burning out.

In a normal, healthy depressed response, your stress hormones also reach high levels, but as you reintegrate and find a creative solution to your difficulty, the levels fall back to normal. If the reintegration doesn't occur, however, as in major depressive disorder, the high levels stay high—"burning out" your bodymind. In that case, your adrenals keep releasing so much epinephrine that soon the stores of it are exhausted, leading you to feel what is sometimes described as "nervous exhaustion," or a "nervous breakdown." Your adrenals keep on manufacturing lots of cortisol, and in fact their production goes into such high gear that it goes out of control, and can't be turned down easily again. Your bodymind becomes unable to stop the process. Such high levels of cortisol in people with major depressive disorder can actually cause damage to their brain cells, making them feel more depressed—and setting up a vicious cycle. This runaway secretion of cortisol can be detected with blood tests, and has been used by doctors to help diagnose major depressive disorder.

Here we have one way in which what is happening in our mind is mirrored by what is happening in our body. When we're unable to turn off our depressed response normally, we are simultaneously also unable to turn off our high output of stress hormones, and vice versa. People to whom this happens have something interfering with the proper completion of their responses—both emotionally and physically. They get "stuck" in stress and depression.

What is the interfering factor? It may be inherited in the genes. In some people, though, it can be due to psychological or social difficulties, or physical illnesses. All of these things can disrupt the functioning of your bodymind.

The good news is that because we now understand the stress response to be a classic bodymind phenomenon, we know that it can be brought back into balance using techniques aimed at any—or all—levels of your being. Physical techniques, like progressive muscle relaxation or exercise (see Chapter 17), can be supplemented and enhanced with a variety of mental stress-stopping techniques (for example, those discussed in Chapters 17 and 18). These exercises have powerful restorative effects on your bodymind, and help to both prevent and treat major depressive disorder.

How Your Brain Handles Stress

The human brain is the most complex structure in the known universe. We are only beginning to learn how it works. We do know, however, much about how your brain works when under stress.

Inside your brain, chemicals are used to send messages from one area to another. We call these chemicals neurotransmitters. Messages about mood are carried mainly by the neurotransmitters serotonin and norepinephrine. They are produced in groups of cells near the base of your brain, and from there they are sent out on nerve pathways throughout the rest of your central nervous system. They are then picked up by other nerve cells through special receptors on the surface of cells. This completes the transmission of the message.

Your levels of serotonin and norepinephrine change as your emotions change. In a very real sense, they are the physical reflections of your emotional state. For example, when you become stressed or anxious, your brain produces increased amounts of serotonin and norepinephrine. Norepinephrine is very similar to the epinephrine produced by your adrenal glands. And like the adrenals' stress hormones, these neurotransmitters help you deal with difficult situations. They make you more alert, boost your mood, and help you prepare to fight or run. Unfortunately, in the same way that your adrenals soon run out of epinephrine, your brain can't keep producing large amounts of these neurotransmitters for long. This is what happens when you become depressed. You need more neurotransmitters, then, to help elevate your mood.

Conventional antidepressant drugs work by increasing the effects of the neurotransmitters. They basically fool your brain into thinking that there is more serotonin and norepinephrine around than there really is. The herb St. John's wort seems to work in this way as well, although it has other antidepressant effects, too (see Chapter 11).

Your brain makes serotonin and norepinephrine out of amino acids supplied in proteins in your diet, and uses various vitamins in the process as well. Because of this, providing the correct supplementary amino acids and vitamins can enable your brain to produce more of these neurotransmitters, nutritionally supporting your brain's own antidepressant mechanisms (see Chapter 12 for details). This is one of the many reasons why attention to nutrition is so important when you're depressed. Another reason is that with nutritional therapy, your immune system can be brought back into balance, and as you'll see below, this has a special relevance for depressed people.

The Immune System and Depression

We all know that when we become emotionally upset we are more susceptible to illness. Recent research has proven this, and has shown that abnormal immune functioning is an important feature of major depressive disorder. The more depressed you are, the more disturbed your immunity is.[1] In fact, this link is so strong that some scientists have even suggested that major depressive disorder is mainly an immunological problem.

In some people with major depressive disorder, their immune system is suppressed, resulting in a low resistance to infections. I very frequently see people with depression who get one cold after another, or recurrent urinary tract infections, sinusitis, and so on.

Other depressed people have *overactive* immune systems— similar to the conditions seen in autoimmune diseases and in some cases of chronic fatigue syndrome. Their whole immune system seems to go haywire, into runaway overdrive. Their white blood cells produce abnormally high levels of interleukins, which are hormones that boost immune responses. They have fewer suppressor T-cells, whose job is normally to dampen down the immune response. Even though they're overactive, the immune systems of depressed people do not function well. The cells do not respond normally; control of their activity seems to have been lost to some degree.[2] This is why subtle immune disorders like allergies, arthritis, or thyroid disease are so common in people with depression.

The immune response in major depressive disorder is very similar to the adrenals' stress-hormone response, and the brain's neurotransmitter response: They all mirror the psychological upset. They all reflect an inability to resolve the bodymind's responses. Unable to be turned off again, they're all in a state of overactivation; of unfocused and unproductive high energy, leading to burnout.

These recent discoveries about the immune systems of depressed people are important because they suggest new ways of treating depression, using natural, nutritionally based, immunologically active therapies, like evening primrose oil, flax oil, and fish oils—as I'll discuss in Chapter 12.

Although the illnesses caused by immune system upsets— like allergies and chronic infections—require specific therapies of their own, they usually improve, or are even cured, by a proper holistic approach to your depression.

So far in this chapter we've taken a look at how stress affects your bodymind. This raises the questions: What brings on such severe stress? What makes you vulnerable to it? It's clear that in order to treat stress and depression properly, we need to find out what led to them in the first place.

How We Become Susceptible to Stress and Depression

What has stressed you out and led to your depression? The answer may seem obvious if you are in a major life crisis. But the obvious answer is hardly ever the only one. In most cases, there are contributing factors.

It's actually not that uncommon for a person to have no idea what is causing her depression. She might not know, for instance, that the stressful things she's experienced, or the way she's dealt with them, have left her vulnerable to depression. She might not be aware of her own inner psychological conflicts, or there might be feelings that she hasn't allowed herself to express consciously. As I mentioned in Chapter 1, a prerequisite for the development of depression is that at least some aspect of the problem the person is facing remains submerged in the subconscious mind. Depression is a sign that there is some issue that needs to be brought to light and dealt with consciously.

To illustrate these points, I'll discuss the case of David, who became depressed after suffering a financial setback. There were many different factors that made him vulnerable to depression, and as you'll see, these needed to be dealt with in his therapy.

David's Story

"I've ended up with nothing again," David said to me. "After all that effort, I'm back to square one." David was thirty-seven years old, and after nearly going bankrupt trying to run a music store, he had just spent his savings on setting himself up in the carpet-cleaning business.

At the time, David had barely enough money to purchase a van, cleaning equipment, and advertising brochures for his business, but he hadn't had enough for the insurance. Only two months after starting work, he skidded off the road into a creek bed. The van was destroyed, and though he wasn't physically injured in the accident, he was broke once more, and very stressed out.

His father had always told him he'd never succeed in life. His mother had been chronically depressed, probably because she was married to such an abusive man. When his father had passed away a few years ago, David had secretly felt glad about it, but also disgusted at himself for feeling that way.

All of these events were a set-up for depression in David. For starters, the kind of neglect or abuse from parents that David experienced makes people more likely to become depressed. People who've been abused usually have conflicting feelings about their parents, as well as some degree of self-hatred, which is a strong promoter of depression. Adding to his risk, though, David also tended to worry a lot, and was introverted and hypersensitive—meaning he had many of the characteristics of what psychologists call the "depression-prone personality."

It wasn't surprising, then, that he developed a depressed response after the accident. Stressful events in life are a common trigger for the response. Other examples of the events that might do this are a relationship breakdown; a change of employment or residence; a recent birth, death, or illness in the family; or a family member leaving home.

We know that the stressful event itself is in many cases less important than the meaning the person reads into it. For example, a change of employment or a divorce can sometimes be seen as positive events, if previous conditions had been intolerable. If the event is seen as reflecting a deep personal defect or failure, however, it is likely to lead to a depressed response.

People who have had difficult childhoods, or who have some deep sense of self-dislike, as David had, often haven't had the chance to develop the degree of trust in themselves and the world they need in order to resolve their depressed responses. And so they often go on to develop major depressive disorder.

As part of his holistic treatment plan, David needed counseling to clarify and start to resolve his issues about his parents, and to deal with his beliefs that he was destined to always be a failure.

In therapy, he discovered that he tended to habitually think of himself and the world in an unrealistic, pessimistic way. This is common in people who are prone to depression. They also tend to blame themselves excessively, and have difficulty expressing their needs. All of this means that they approach things with an unhealthy degree of passivity and helplessness. Of course, these are generalizations, but it is surprising how frequently this is the case. (For a discussion of ways of identifying and changing unrealistic, negative beliefs and raising self-esteem, see Chapter 18.)

In addition to counseling, David began an exercise program (see Chapter 17) as well as some basic nutritional therapy (Chapters 12 and 13). He also enrolled in a community college with the help of financial aid, learning computer skills to enhance his employability. Taking active steps to deal with sources of chronic stress like unemployment or social isolation is one of the most important ways to emotionally strengthen oneself.

Like David, most people who develop depression have some source of chronic stress in their lives. Apart from unemployment or loneliness, this might include ill health, boredom, overwork, or other sources of dissatisfaction. The feeling that their life is not turning out the way they had hoped it would is very common. Again, the meaning the source of chronic stress has to the person is more important than the source itself. If the person blames himself for it or feels powerless to do anything about it, he is far more likely to become depressed than if he continues to make active efforts to overcome the problem.

Social isolation is an especially serious cause of chronic stress. The fewer social interactions and supports a person has, the more vulnerable she is to feeling down. Any doctor will tell you that they see patients who are socially isolated far more frequently than other patients. They are genuinely sicker than others, too. Put simply, prolonged isolation causes your bodymind to break down. We all need somebody to confide in. In Chapter 18, you'll find a discussion of how to start to incorporate the healing advantages of social connectedness into your life.

Is Depression in the Genes?

David had another important factor that predisposed him to major depressive disorder: a family history of the illness. There is still some disagreement in the psychiatric profession about why the susceptibility to developing major depressive disorder runs in families. Is it due to genetics, or is it due to psychological and social effects? Experts believe that all of these factors are involved, but that the psychological and social influences are much more important than the genetic ones. Genes on their own have only a very weak effect on depression.

What this means is that although people worry that they will pass the illness on to their children through their genes, all they can really pass on in this way is the *susceptibility* to it. It takes other factors, like severe stress, to actually bring on the illness in those who are susceptible. This is what happened to David. It also means that if there's a history of major depressive disorder in your family, it's not at all inevitable that you'll get it. If you take steps to look after your physical and emotional health—say, by eating a good diet, exercising, getting regular sunlight, meditating, staying socially connected, respecting your depressed responses, and so on—you'll strengthen your bodymind to the point where you can resolve your responses normally, and not develop major depressive disorder.

Searching for the Causes of Your Depression

Most people who become depressed do not have as many predisposing factors as David did. It's always worth searching for them, though. This is important, since your therapy should be tailored to specifically address any underlying vulnerabilities you may have, so that you will be less likely to become ill again. Unfortunately, most conventional physicians do not do this. They believe it's enough just to suppress the symptoms of depression with drugs. As I explained in Chapter 1, this only makes patients more likely to become depressed in the future.

Preferably, your therapist should be aware of the causes that can exist on every level of your being. It's a shame, for instance, that a few psychologists ignore the physical causes of depression, just as some physicians ignore the psychological causes. Holistically minded physicians are the ones who are most capable of dealing with all of the levels of a person's being, as I'll discuss in Chapter 9.

Another reason that it's important to be able to address both mind and body in therapy is that depression is associated with many physical illnesses—illnesses that patients are often unaware they have. In the next chapter, I'll discuss these illnesses, and the steps you can take to deal with them naturally.

✦

CHAPTER 8

MEDICAL MYSTERY TOUR

The excursion is the same when you go looking for your
sorrow as when you go looking for your joy.
—*EUDORA WELTY*

Proper Diagnosis: An Essential

IT seems simple. If you feel depressed, you must be suffering from depression, right?

Unfortunately, it's not as straightforward as that. There are literally dozens of medical conditions that can cause feelings of depression, any one of which you might have but not be aware of. Furthermore, you might not realize that the over-the-counter or prescription drugs you may be taking can also cause depression. Your bodymind's hormonal and immunological mechanisms for resolving the depressed response can be disrupted by many medical conditions and drugs, giving rise to major depressive disorder. These hidden causes of depression are much more common than most people suspect.

Therefore, when you go to a doctor with symptoms of depression, there needs to be a careful search for underlying conditions. That's why it's so important that you consult a medical doctor before you consult with a therapist—a therapist without a medical degree can sometimes overlook physiological causes of depression. You should have a full history and physical examination done, and a set of standard laboratory tests.

In this chapter I'll discuss some of the more common conditions that either cause or are associated with depression. I'll tell you how they're recognized, and what you can do about them.

The Forgotten Endocrine Causes

Many depressed people have *thyroid disease,* but the diagnosis is missed because their doctors forget to check for it. The thyroid is a regulator of the body's metabolic rate, and when it malfunctions, the person either speeds up or slows down. In *hypothyroidism,* the thyroid gland fails to produce enough thyroid hormone, and so the metabolic rate slows—like a clock that hasn't been rewound. Such people may become tired, constipated, and sensitive to cold. They might put on weight, and have vague aches and pains throughout the body. They might have irregular periods. They also tend to become forgetful and depressed. Sometimes, however, the only symptom of hypothyroidism is depression, so it is essential that every person with depression receive a blood test for their thyroid function.

Hypothyroidism is easily treated with thyroid hormone tablets, and this may completely cure the depression. In fact, thyroid hormone tablets are so effective that sometimes psychiatrists use them in patients with severe depression even if their thyroid function is normal. Naturopaths also sometimes use thyroid hormones to treat depression, as well as many other conditions. Incidentally, *hyperthyroidism* (too much thyroid hormone) can also cause depression, although it is less likely.

Premenstrual syndrome (PMS) includes symptoms of depression—restlessness, irritability, and tension. What sets it apart is its distinctive symptom of fluid retention. Some studies have shown that up to 90 percent of women experience recurrent PMS. In classic cases, its symptoms occur in the second half of the menstrual cycle; the first week of the cycle is symptom-free.

The boundaries of PMS blur into those of depression, since depression also tends to get worse premenstrually. The treatment of PMS also overlaps with that of depression. Light therapy, conventional antidepressants, and the herb St. John's wort (see Chapter 11) are all effective to some degree, though hormonal therapy is more commonly used. PMS responds best to a holistic approach incorporating lifestyle modification, nutritional medicine, and other bodymind therapies, such as meditation and visualization.

Postpartum depression is another important endocrine cause. It is associated with the major changes in the levels of hormones that follow childbirth. Problems with other endocrine glands, like the adrenals, pituitary, or parathyroid, can also cause depression. Although they can often be detected by a good routine assessment, specialized blood tests are sometimes required to pick them up.

I know of a woman who had been depressed for over twenty years, and who had been treated by many different psychiatrists with little success, until her family doctor noticed that she had never had her blood calcium level checked. When he checked it, he found it was elevated, and this led to the discovery that she had a disorder of the parathyroid glands—*hyperparathyroidism.* When this was treated surgically, her depression was cured. Every patient with depression should have their calcium level measured as part of their routine lab tests. Unfortunately, this is another commonly forgotten point.

The Depression/Immune Disorder Link

The immune system has strong links with the mind and the emotions, and problems with immunity go hand in hand with depression.

Chronic fatigue syndrome, for example, is due to a disordered immune response, often triggered by a viral infection. The Epstein-

Barr virus is a common culprit, but many other viruses have been implicated. It causes a fatigue so severe that it does not get better with bed rest. Painful lymph nodes, a sore throat, and weakness are some of its other symptoms, as are muscle soreness, headache, and poor sleep. Irritability and depression are common with it, too. In fact, many psychiatrists actually consider chronic fatigue syndrome to be a form of depression. But most now accept it as a distinct disorder. Still, it seems to partly overlap with depression, and in some cases it's hard to tell them apart. Interestingly, many cases of depression are also associated with an abnormal immune response to Epstein-Barr virus infection.[1]

To be blunt, conventional medicine does not have a great deal to offer people with chronic fatigue syndrome. One young man with the syndrome I treated had also been under the care of both an immunologist and a psychiatrist. The psychiatrist, noting the man's abnormal blood tests, had sent him off to the immunologist. The immunologist thought he was just depressed, and so sent him back to the psychiatrist—who, of course, treated him with antidepressant drugs, which didn't help him. This sort of shuffling around is pretty typical of what chronic fatigue syndrome patients experience, and is a result of conventional medicine's inability to see patients in an integrated, bodymind way.

One way to see chronic fatigue syndrome is as a state of being "stuck" in the fatigue response, much as major depressive disorder is a state of being stuck in the depressed response. The fatigue response can be potentially helpful—creating a static or still period of time to gather energy or inner resources for the next life step. But if it doesn't resolve, it is no longer helpful—it becomes an illness. Another way to see chronic fatigue syndrome is as the result of a deep-seated crisis involving the person's will and life-energy. Many patients are also in the process of coping with major spiritual issues. As with PMS, I recommend natural therapies.

Other chronic immune disorders and infections are also associated with depression, including *HIV* and *tuberculosis*. If you have had unprotected sex in the last ten years or so, or have shared a needle, I strongly recommend that you have an HIV test.

Chronic overgrowth of the yeast *Candida* albicans has also been claimed by many to cause depression. Candida lives in limited numbers on the skin and in the digestive tract of most people; if their immunity weakens, or if they use antibiotics or oral contraceptives, candida can proliferate to become a serious problem. It can also occasionally become a problem if a person develops an allergy to it. Itchy rashes occur on the skin or in the vagina, sometimes with painful white patches in the mouth. In some people, the symptoms are vague and are spread throughout the body. Headache, difficulty concentrating, anxiety, and depression are some symptoms that are described.[2]

Candidiasis is treated with antifungal medications and acidophilus supplementation (a friendly form of bacteria found in yogurt with real culture, or on its own in powder or tablet form), along with nutritional supplements and a low-yeast diet. Some people have had excellent results with this treatment, though I've found that most people who try it are disappointed. In fact, I've seen a patient become more depressed after going on a yeast-free diet. I believe candidiasis is a less common cause of depression than has been claimed.

Autoimmune disorders including *systemic lupus erythematosus* (SLE) and *rheumatoid arthritis* are also associated with depression, and I've seen quite a few patients with this combination of illnesses. Women are much more susceptible than men to these types of disorders. In SLE, the woman produces antibodies to her own DNA, leading to damage to cells throughout her body. She often ends up with rashes in sun-exposed areas, patches of hair loss, joint pain, mouth ulcers, and kidney damage. Some women have only subtle symptoms. If SLE is present, the standard screening blood tests for depression will usually be abnormal.

As with many chronic conditions, conventional medicine is frustratingly poor for dealing with autoimmune disorders. If you have one, you would do well to visit a clinical ecologist, naturopath, or other practitioner of holistic medicine, who can offer you many effective modalities of treatment. One of the rewards of practicing natural medicine comes from seeing patients with autoimmune disorders recover their health by using simple natural methods—such as a supervised detoxification program, visualization techniques, and lifestyle changes—after their conventional doctors had told them there was nothing left to offer them except dangerous immune-suppressing drugs.

The Migraine/Depression Link

I've found that a very high percentage of the people I've treated for depression—perhaps 50 percent or so—also have migraines, and when both conditions are present, each seems to make the other worse. Both problems share certain biochemical features, including a disturbance of serotonin metabolism, and treatment for one condition often helps the other.

I've also noticed that people with severe migraines tend to have an unusual sort of inner lifestyle. They go through buildup periods of intense, driven emotions or mental activity, followed by a migraine, which then forces them to stop and rest. This enforced break seems to reset the cycle, until the stressors in their lives start the buildup again.

The most dramatic example of this that I've seen was in the case of a depressed young woman who was driven by feelings of guilt for having survived when her sister died of cancer in childhood. She felt determined to "make her life count" to justify her existence. A law student, she also simultaneously held two part-time jobs and volunteered in a number of charity organizations, often working until four in the morning. She would go through cycles of increasing emotional and physical stress until she had one of her regular migraines—so severe that they literally paralyzed her for a day at a time. She had tried all the various preventive medications for migraines, but none had helped. I believe her migraines were resistant to treatment because she needed them so badly—they were the only way she felt she could justify resting and spending some time focusing on her own needs.

If the migraine-inducing stressors in a person's life cannot be changed, it's important that he or she learn alternative methods of coping with them. The issues involved usually have to do with interpersonal relations of some sort, and courses in communication skills, assertiveness training, self-esteem, and relaxation can be of benefit. I also like to prescribe physiotherapy or other types of bodywork, as well as the herb feverfew *(Chrysanthemum parthenium)*, which has been proven in a placebo-controlled trial to be effective in migraine prevention.[3] (PLEASE NOTE: Feverfew should not be taken by pregnant women or anyone who has a blood clotting disorder.) Caffeine and cigarettes should be eliminated, and a search for food allergies is worthwhile as well.

A variety of other brain disorders, like *head injuries* or *epilepsy,* can in some cases cause depression. *Stroke, cancer,* and *dementia* can usually be ruled out with a history and neurological examination, though in some cases a CT scan of the head is necessary, especially in older patients. A person having a stroke usually experiences a "funny turn" of some sort—like an episode of confusion, visual disturbance, slurred speech, weakness, dizziness, or numbness. Such people also usually have histories of high blood pressure or heart disease.

Most people have worried that they've had a brain tumor at some stage in their lives, but fortunately, tumors are a very uncommon cause of depression. They classically cause a headache that is worse at night, along with symptoms of brain damage, such as partial blindness, loss of speech, weakness or numbness, or seizures.

Another disease many people at one time or another worry that they might have is dementia. There is an old medical saying that holds true, though: People who *complain* of loss of memory have depression, not dementia. People who really have dementia often do not pay much attention to their memory loss.

Mimics of Depression

Chronic pain syndromes of all types are strongly linked to depression. Physical pain causes depression, and depression can also cause physical pain. Unquestionably, pain is both an emotional and a physical experience. I've seen case after case where people with chronic pain have gone through the whole route of medications, acupuncture, nerve blocks, and even repeated operations to finally experience relief only when the emotional aspects of their lives are brought into the therapy.

Chronic diseases of any sort can also cause or predispose to depression, including *heart disease* and *kidney failure*. Anemia causes symptoms of tiredness, weakness, insomnia, dizziness, pounding heartbeat, and shortness of breath, and can mimic depression. The history, examination, and blood tests that a good physician will do for a patient with depression are designed to rule out these causes of depression.

Dietary, Lifestyle, and Environmental Causes of Depression

What you eat can have powerful effects on your mood. A diet high in refined and synthetic foods can predispose you to depression. *Vitamin deficiencies* can also cause depression. In Chapters 12 and 13, I discuss these topics in depth—and tell you how healthy food can help lift your spirits. *Food allergies,* a controversial but potentially important cause, is also discussed there. Poisoning by a variety of *environmental pollutants,* like lead in the drinking water, can also cause or contribute to depression, and is discussed in Chapter 14.

Other lifestyle and environmental factors also impact on depression, such as a *lack of adequate sunlight, exercise, or play.* Having seen the therapeutic effects that bringing these factors back into balance can have, I've learned that one cannot underestimate their importance. I'll tell you how you can take advantage of their healing power in Chapters 15 and 17.

Substance Abuse: Bitter Living Through Chemistry

Alcohol, sleeping tablets, sedatives like Valium, painkillers, speed, cocaine, and marijuana can all cause depression. In many cases, the depression comes first; the person then attempts to make himself feel better by getting drunk or high. Addictions are often a way of trying to escape from the transformative work of the depressed response, as I discussed in Chapter 6. Yet they only put a further strain on the body's biochemistry, and eventually the depression worsens, often very severely. In fact, the worst cases of depression are quite often related to substance abuse.

A lot of people still cling to the belief that *marijuana* is totally harmless, in spite of a huge and growing body of scientific evidence against this. It may be less harmful than alcohol, but I have seen too many cases of mental illness in heavy marijuana smokers to retain any illusions about it. Many people who are diagnosed with schizophrenia, I believe, have nothing other than chronic marijuana poisoning. Despite this, marijuana can be a valuable medication in certain instances, such as for the treatment of cancer-induced loss of appetite.

Unlike the case of marijuana, most people are aware of the dangers of smoking *tobacco.* But they may be unaware of its association with depression and other mental illnesses. People with mental illness are the heaviest smokers you'll find. This is because nicotine activates the brain's reward mechanism, providing a temporary boost to mood. Nicotine is the most addictive substance known—ask any former heroin addict. They'll tell you that giving up heroin is easy compared to cigarettes. Add to that the fact that a wide variety of substances in cigarette smoke arc toxic to nerve cells. For example, *heterocyclic amines* in smoke disrupt metabolic processes, including the production of neurotransmitters. Chronic exposure to cigarette smoke is thus linked to depression.[4]

Caffeine also ranks as an addictive psychoactive drug, even though it remains quite socially acceptable. It interferes with brain chemistry by stopping the enzyme phosphodiesterase from working, causing a buildup of what are essentially metabolic waste products. Cells are forced into a stimulated state, leading to its alerting effects. Caffeine and its breakdown products remain in the body long after the initial alerting effect has worn off. Because of this, many people are unaware that their morning coffee is the cause of their difficulty in sleeping at night. Research has shown that caffeine use is also linked to depression in some individuals, as well as anxiety and fatigue.[5]

Is Your Medicine Giving You the Blues?

Doctors sometimes overlook medications as a cause of depression. A surprising number of over-the-counter and prescription drugs have a powerful depressant effect in many people. Here is a list of the more common ones:

Analgesics: ibuprofen and indomethacin, and opioids like codeine and dextropropoxyphene
Anticonvulsants: phenytoin, carbamazepine
Antihypertensives and cardiac drugs: beta-blockers (especially propranolol), digoxin
Antipsychotics: fluphenazine, chlorpromazine, trifluoperazine, haloperidol, and others.
Sedatives and hypnotics: diazepam, oxazepam, temazepam, clonazepam, lorazepam, and others

Steroids: oral contraceptives, corticosteroids (though steroid ointments are unlikely to be absorbed well enough to cause depression), and anabolic steroids
Vitamins, minerals, and other supplements: megadoses of vitamin A and D (e.g., in cod liver oil), calcium, lecithin

This is only a partial list. You should discuss any medication you may be taking with your doctor to find out if it might be affecting your mood.

Is It Really Depression—Or Is It Something Else?

A doctor seeing a depressed person needs to make sure that what the person has is, in fact, depression and not a different mental condition. Sometimes this isn't as obvious as you might think. A number of different mental disorders have features similar to depression, or can lead to the development of depression. They include bipolar disorder (also called manic-depression), dysthymia, anxiety disorders, eating disorders, and schizophrenia.

People with *bipolar disorder* usually have episodes of depression, but they also have periods of abnormally elevated or irritable mood, and overactivity. The treatment of bipolar disorder is different from depression and usually includes mood-stabilizing drugs like lithium or carbamazepine.

Dysthymia is the term psychiatrists use to describe a type of depression that is low level and constant, and therefore does not meet the full criteria for major depressive disorder. It is also so chronic (lasting two years or more) that it is considered to be a personality style rather than an illness as such. Despite this, it is often treated as an illness, using the same therapies as for depression. This is a good idea, since people with dysthymia frequently have episodes of major depressive disorder. (Psychiatrists sometimes call this "double depression.")

People with *anxiety* and *eating disorders* also frequently become depressed. On the other hand, people with depression are often very anxious, and often have disordered eating—so there is a lot of overlap in these conditions. Psychiatrists like to use antidepressants to treat all of them. Psychologically based treatments, such as counseling from a skilled therapist, are sometimes much more effective than drugs for anxiety or eating disorders.

Schizophrenia includes symptoms of delusions (false beliefs that the person insists are true, no matter what the evidence against them is) and hallucinations (hearing voices and seeing things that aren't really there). The person also tends to lose interest in the outside world and becomes depressed. Antipsychotic drugs like haloperidol and fluphenazine are used to treat schizophrenia. Unfortunately, a side effect is depression! So again, there is a lot of overlap, and sometimes making the distinction between schizophrenia and depression is difficult.

A Medical Mystery Tour

As you can see, making an accurate diagnosis of depression is anything but straightforward. For this reason, I once more encourage you to seek medical assistance if you have symptoms of depression. In the next part of the book, I'll discuss ways of finding the right person to help you, and how you can integrate alternative and conventional medicine into your own personalized treatment plan.

✦

PART III

Healing Your Bodymind: Holistic Medicine for Major Depressive Disorder

The healing path is made up of the steps we take to enact our own potential—steps that may lead into every region of our lives. For if the roots of disease are multifactorial, then healing, too, must be manifold. . . . If sickness echoes through the concentric circles of our existence, then healing, too, must reverberate everywhere.

—MARC IAN BARASCH

✦

CHAPTER 9

ON FINDING A THERAPIST

Give sorrow words; the grief that does not speak
Whispers the o'er-fraught heart and bids it break.
—WILLIAM SHAKESPEARE

Words are a form of action, capable of influencing
change.—INGRID BENGIS

PROBABLY the single most powerful protective factor against depression is the presence of someone to confide in. The more close and caring relationships we have with other people, the less likely we are to become depressed.

Our society has become increasingly fragmented socially. Despite all the advancements of mass communication, most of us are emotionally isolated, lacking the rich social support networks that people in preindustrial societies took for granted. People once lived in close contact with their extended families, with several generations under one roof. They grew up with their neighbors and knew most of the people in their town.

Today we enjoy an unprecedented degree of personal independence, but it comes with a hefty price tag. When we need help, we often find we're alone, and end up having to rely on professionals and their impersonal institutions. Therapists have come to fill the role of our confidants.

Who to Consult First

Although they may not practice natural or holistic medicine, a general practitioner (GP) or family physician is probably the best person to consult first. He or she will be aware of and look for the physical illnesses or drugs that could be responsible for your depression, and will be able to determine how severe your depression is. If necessary, she might refer you to a psychiatrist. Most people who are depressed, however, are treated by family doctors. Often the best medicine is practiced by local family doctors, since they know their patients well and are generally available at short notice if problems arise. I encourage you to find a family doctor to whom you feel you can talk, who listens to you, and then stick with her.

Finding a doctor who practices according to the principles of natural medicine may require some extra effort. A good place to start is by contacting the American Holistic Medical Association and asking for a listing of holistic medical practitioners in your area. (The address and phone number is in Appendix 1.) If you are fortunate enough to live in one of the states where naturopaths (N.D.'s) are licensed—and the number of such states is steadily growing—you will have access to one of the new generation of naturopaths trained in accredited schools. Formerly, the profession of naturopathic medicine was unregulated, but these days licensed naturopaths in the United States have received a high level of education. Contact the American Association of Naturopathic Physicians to find one near you (see Appendix 1).

By shopping around, you may be able to find a GP, naturopathic physician, or a psychiatrist who is willing to do counseling/psychotherapy with you, and maybe even one who has an awareness of some of the alternative treatment options discussed in this book. Show him this book or discuss it with him. Even if he's not familiar with all the treatment options, most doctors are happy to use therapies that have been scientifically demonstrated to be effective.

If your chosen doctor does not do counseling/psychotherapy, it's important that you find someone who does—either someone specializing in counseling for you to see in addition to your doctor, like a psychologist, or another doctor who can be your sole treatment provider.

Choosing a Counselor

To write prescriptions is easy, but to come to an understanding with people is hard.
—*FRANZ KAFKA*

Laura Davis, the author of *The Courage to Heal Workbook,* writes: "One of the most important support people you can have while you're healing is a skilled counselor. A good counselor provides hope, insight, information, and consistent loving support as you go through the healing process. By encouraging you to develop the capacity to heal yourself, effective counselors work themselves out of a job. Because they are not directly involved in your life, counselors have a unique point of view that can be a powerful catalyst for healing."[1]

Before choosing a therapist, ask friends, family members or people who have been in therapy for names of therapists. Contact various health agencies or organizations who may be able to put you in touch with the services you need. Remember that it's likely you will need to "shop" for a counselor or have initial sessions with several until you find the person who fits your requirements and, most of all, with whom you feel comfortable and can trust.

Davis elaborates:

When you're looking for a counselor, it's helpful to take the attitude that you are a consumer making an informed choice about the person you're hiring to work with you. Even though you're seeking counseling to fill an emotional need, you are still paying for a service. Being a consumer gives you certain rights:

The right to determine the qualities you want in your
   therapist
The right to choose a therapist who meets your needs
The right to be heard, believed, and treated with respect
The right to say no to any suggestions your therapist
   makes
The right to be satisfied by the services you're receiving
The right to freely discuss any problems that arise in
   therapy with your counselor
The right to end a therapy relationship that isn't work-
   ing for you.[2]

The Way of the Psychiatrist

Say the word *psychiatry* to people and they will exhibit a vague
sense of unease. What goes through their minds are images of
people kept against their will in straitjackets and padded cells,
receiving shock treatment from doctors and nurses who are
themselves barely sane. Book after book on the evils of psychiatry stock the shelves of bookstores and public libraries. Alternative therapists, especially, often tend to see the profession of
psychiatry as some sort of conspiracy against humanity by the
multinational medical-industrial complex.

   Unfortunately, mental illness and everything associated with
it have always made people feel uneasy, and what they feel uneasy
about, they demonize. Having worked in psychiatric hospitals,
though, I know that, in general, psychiatrists and psychiatric
nurses are people who are as caring and concerned for the wel-
fare of others as you are likely to find anywhere. In treating people with severe, chronic mental illness, they are caring for those
society often ignores. I don't know of a single place in the world
where public psychiatric services are adequately funded by the
government. Many people with schizophrenia, even in the
United States, receive no medical care and live in cardboard

boxes, eating out of Dumpsters, because the rest of society is simply not concerned about them.

Psychiatry has also been accused of dehumanizing people by treating them as though their problems were completely biochemical. To some extent this criticism is a valid one. Psychiatrists do tend to see their patients as walking biochemical problems, and their job as being mainly one of selecting the right drug. Often, medication is the sole treatment offered. Psychological causes of mental illness are acknowledged, but generally disregarded, through lack of interest or lack of resources, since psychotherapy is usually more expensive than medication.

In fact, psychiatry is probably more biochemically oriented, as opposed to psychologically oriented, than any other branch of medicine. This may sound strange, but it is the logical outcome of events in psychiatry over the last forty years, since the first successful drug treatments for mental illnesses were introduced. Until that time, psychiatry was considered totally unscientific by the rest of the medical profession. Psychoanalysis, for example, rested on unprovable assumptions about fanciful things like the id and the superego. You could not put things like that under a microscope or in a test tube, so hardheaded scientists scoffed at them.

When effective drugs became available, psychiatrists took that ball and ran with it. They've been running ever since, trying to prove that their treatments are real and physical, just like the other branches of medicine. This inferiority complex has meant that psychiatry is now mainly biochemically oriented.

This physical focus has had some positive effects. It has removed from patients and their families any blame for the illness. For example, in the 1950s, schizophrenia was commonly believed by psychiatrists to be caused by faulty mothering. I'm sure that belief led to a lot of grief among mothers of people with schizophrenia. Nowadays, the blame is put on genetic, viral, and biochemical causes—more morally neutral territory.

When a Psychiatrist Can Help

There are times when psychiatric help can be lifesaving. Anyone whose depression is severe or is not responding to basic therapies should see a psychiatrist. Suicidal feelings are a clear indication that help should be sought straightaway, if necessary from the local hospital's emergency room. A short stay in a hospital can give a person enough time away from life's difficulties to break the cycle of depression and approach the situation anew.

There are a growing number of psychiatrists who understand the importance of a holistic approach, so again, I encourage you to ask and shop around for someone you are really satisfied with.

CHAPTER 10

✦

THE PLACE FOR MEDICATION

CONVENTIONAL antidepressant medication or alternative medicine—which is better?

The answer is that they are both useful, and it is not really an either/or situation. Each has its place. Most people who use alternative medicine also see a conventional doctor for the same condition. There doesn't need to be any conflict between the two methods of healing; in fact, they can complement and enhance each other's functions. Whatever style of medicine your current therapist practices, you deserve to learn about all the available options for your treatment.

These days, the distinction between conventional and alternative medicine is becoming increasingly blurred. For example, conventional researchers are discovering more and more about the uses of nutritional medicine, a field that was once considered to be almost entirely alternative. There is now also conventional research, for instance, on meditation that shows it to be effective for some conditions. There's even a dawning awareness in the United States of the effectiveness of some herbal medications. In Germany, herbal medicine already *is* conventional medicine. It is taught in medical schools as part of the standard curriculum, and 80 percent of German doctors now prescribe herbs. Someday, this will probably occur here, too.

In my opinion, doctors who practice holistic medicine— that is, those who are combining conventional and alternative approaches—are really just doing what all doctors will eventually do.

When Antidepressant Medications Can Help

If you go to a conventional doctor for help with depression today, you are virtually guaranteed to be prescribed a synthetic antidepressant drug. This may or may not be the best thing for you.

I am not ideologically opposed to the use of antidepressant drugs—on the contrary, I see drugs as being as valid as any other form of treatment, such as psychological or spiritual therapies. That is what "holistic" really means: accepting the whole situation, the whole person. Just as we are beings who think and have a soul, we are also beings whose bodies have a biochemical basis, treatable with drugs.

Even from a purely spiritual perspective, drugs can be a valid form of treatment. In his *Tales of the Hasidim*, for example, Martin Buber recounted the following story:

> Once Rabbi Barukh went to the city and bought medicine for his sick daughter. He set it on the window-sill of his room. . . . Rabbi Barukh went up and down, looked at the little bottles, and said: ". . . But why does one give poisons to the sick?"
>
> And answered: "The 'sparks' that fell from the primeval shattering of the worlds into the 'shells' and penetrated the stuff of stones, plants, and animals—all ascend back to their source through the sanctification of the devout people who work at them, use them, and consume them in holiness. But how shall those sparks that fell into bitter poisons be redeemed? That they might not remain in exile, God appointed them for the sick: to each the carriers of the sparks which belong to the root of their soul. Thus the sick are themselves physicians who heal the poisons."

I am opposed, however, to the *overuse* of drugs. People who are having a normal and healthy depressed response, as described in Part 1 of this book, should not be treated with anti-depressant drugs, since they can disrupt the process. But if their depressed response goes wrong and turns into major depressive disorder, that's another story altogether. Major depressive disorder is not a normal or healthy thing. It is a process that should be interrupted, and therefore drugs become an important therapeutic option for it.

In those cases, conventional antidepressant drugs can be indispensable. They can help the severely depressed in times when they're literally too depressed for other kinds of therapy. In severe depression, a person might not be able to concentrate enough for psychotherapy or even relaxation therapy. Or they might have tried all the other treatments with limited effect, and in getting over the obstacle might need an extra push. Antidepressant drugs are a very effective form of treatment, and have probably saved hundreds of thousands of lives.

Yet even in severe depression, drugs should not be the *only* treatment used. Good conventional psychiatrists know this. If the patient is capable of it, psychotherapy—and in many cases, family therapy—should be offered. Attention should also be paid to the person's lifestyle, whether he is getting enough exercise, a nutritious diet, and so on. Only when all the factors in the his life that contributed to his depression have been dealt with can a treatment really be said to have been adequate. And only then will a relapse of depression be unlikely to occur.

If you're taking medication, you can complement it with many other forms of treatment, giving yourself a much more powerful overall antidepressant effect. In the chapters that follow, I'll discuss the benefits of nutritional therapy, sunlight, exercise, cognitive therapy, and other forms of healing. You can also use the therapies I described earlier in the book, like dream therapy, art therapy, and exercises in creative problem solving. The only treatments in this book that you should *not* mix with con-

ventional medications are the herbal antidepressant St. John's
wort and amino acid supplements.

Antidepressant medications need to be taken seriously and
cautiously. Despite recent improvements, they still have many
side effects, some of which can be severe. Because of their side
effects, I believe that, in general, they should be reserved for people with moderate-to-severe depression.

It's important that you learn about a drug's effects and side
effects, for your own safety. I've often been surprised at how little people know about the drugs they're taking. In this chapter,
I'll go through some basic information about the commonly
used drug options.

The Choices in Conventional Medications

There are three main types of conventional antidepressant medications: SSRIs like Prozac and Zoloft; cyclic antidepressants,
including Tofranil and Elavil; and MAOIs like Parnate and
Nardil. There are other types, too, including Desyrel, Wellbutrin,
and Effexor. In addition, many new drugs have recently been
developed, and they may well make these other choices obsolete
in the next decade or so.

Each type of drug has a different set of side effects, but they
all share some common characteristics: They relieve the symptoms of depression in 60 to 80 percent of people who use them,
and they take four to six weeks to produce their full effects.

The different groups of antidepressants each affect a slightly
different set of chemicals in your brain. Since the chemistry of
each person's brain is unique, you might do better with one type
of drug than you would with the others. Usually, it's a matter of
trial and error to find the one that's right for you. If a given drug
is going to be helpful, it should have produced a beneficial effect
by the fourth week or so. If it hasn't worked by then, a different
drug can be tried.

The choice of which one to use first is usually based on which set of side effects you are willing to put up with. If you're very restless at night, for instance, you might be more willing to take Desyrel, since it causes drowsiness. You will probably not want Prozac, because it can make restlessness worse. This is the sort of reasoning psychiatrists use when they prescribe antidepressants.

Antidepressants produce their effects in an interesting way: They start with your body, and then only gradually begin to affect your mind and emotions. So the first symptoms to improve—usually starting around the tenth day—are your physical symptoms, like fatigue, insomnia, and loss of appetite. Then your low mood begins to lift.

Prozac and the Other SSRIs

SSRIs (serotonin-specific reuptake inhibitors) like Prozac (fluoxetine) or Zoloft (sertraline) are currently recommended as first-line drugs. Prozac, introduced in 1988, has become the most widely used antidepressant in the United States. Actually, classifying it as an antidepressant is a little misleading. It is used not only for the treatment of depression but for a wide range of other psychiatric problems, including eating disorders, anxiety disorders, and even personality disorders. In addition, many people who are taking it do not really have a psychiatric illness. They use it as a means to help them adapt to the stresses of everyday life, although this type of use is not officially sanctioned.

In recent years, attention has focused on the possible ability of Prozac to change people's personality toward becoming more extroverted and confident.[1] This may or may not be true. Many believe it is a placebo effect. Prozac affects the serotonin system in your brain, however, and we know that serotonin is important for how your brain handles social behavior. Altering your levels of serotonin with drugs like Prozac may make you feel less sensitive to rejection, and more willing to take social risks. Our society rewards people who are social risk-takers—outgoing and thick-skinned, like many salespeople and movie stars. That's one of the reasons why Prozac is so popular.

SSRIs like Prozac are sometimes referred to as "low-toxicity" antidepressants. In reality, they are low toxicity only when compared to the older types of antidepressants, which were very toxic indeed. Prozac has many side effects, some of which are severe. In fact, I've seen more than one patient who was seriously poisoned by Prozac.

Let me tell you the story of a fifty-six-year-old woman I treated back in my hospital intern days. She had been admitted to the ward in a state of acute confusion. She was unable to give an account of herself—not knowing where or even who she was, and muttering strange, nonsensical fragments of sentences. She was also completely unable to pass urine. A full examination and set of blood tests and other investigations had been performed, but all the tests had come up normal. Her illness was a mystery. It seemed to be a toxic state of some sort, but what the toxin was we could not establish.

We were able to obtain her name, date of birth, and address from her purse, but that was all the information we had about her. Her neighbors didn't know her. I called around to all the doctors in her area, and finally was able to locate a GP who knew her. He was quite surprised to hear that she was in the hospital.

"Why, yes," he said, "I saw her just recently. She'd been feeling quite depressed over the last few weeks since her son died—and I started her on Prozac ten days ago. . . ."

Bingo. She was suffering from the toxic effects of a so-called low-toxicity antidepressant, which had, incidentally, been prescribed inappropriately in the first place—for a normal grief reaction. Grief is not an illness; it is a natural response, a process that needs to be worked through. I would only consider it abnormal if it was still severely distressing or disabling after a year or so. The pharmaceutical companies, however, and a lot of doctors considered to be experts in antidepressant prescribing, will tell you that antidepressants are indicated even in cases where there is a clear reason for feeling upset, as in this woman's case.

Fortunately, this woman recovered completely after a few days in the hospital. I should point out that reactions as severe as hers are relatively unusual with this drug, although I've seen a few of them.

The common side effects of SSRIs are (using Prozac as an example): nausea (in 21 percent of cases), headache (20 percent), nervousness (15 percent), insomnia (14 percent), weight loss (13 percent), drowsiness (12 percent), diarrhea (12 percent), dry mouth (10 percent), loss of appetite, anxiety, tremor, dizziness, stomach upset, and excessive sweating (all less than 10 percent). Less common side effects include loss of the ability to have an orgasm, the development of various types of rashes, and a decrease in blood glucose (therefore diabetics should use it with care).[2] Recently it's been discovered that Prozac also decreases the body's melatonin levels, which is a worry, considering melatonin not only keeps our body clock regular but also has an important anticancer effect.[3]

In the late 1980s there were widely publicized reports that Prozac was linked to an increased likelihood of violent acts— suicide and homicide—but many subsequent reviews have clearly proved that no such association exists.[4]

Tofranil and the Other Cyclics

The cyclic group of antidepressants, which include Tofranil (imipramine), Elavil (amitriptyline), and Sinequan (doxepin), are the oldest group in use, dating back to the 1950s. Tofranil is still considered to represent the "gold standard" in antidepressant effectiveness—all others are compared to it to determine how well they work.

In terms of side effects, unfortunately, the cyclic antidepressants have by far the worst record. They cause serious side effects with monotonous regularity, especially in patients over the age of sixty-five. Because they interfere with the control of blood pressure, they frequently cause blackouts, which can result in falls and hip fractures. The drowsiness they cause also leads to accidents, and makes it risky to drive or operate heavy machinery. In some patients, they also cause serious abnormalities of the heart's rhythm.

Despite all this, the tricyclics are still the standard type of antidepressant used by many doctors, mainly because they're inexpensive. HMO's, especially, encourage their use as a cost-cutting measure.

The common side effects of the cyclic antidepressants vary from drug to drug, but in general they are, in rough order of occurrence from most frequent to least: sedation, dry mouth and postural hypotension (which causes dizziness on standing up, and may lead to blackouts and falls), nausea, constipation or diarrhea, weight gain, blurred vision, difficulty with urination, increased heart rate, palpitations, sweating, rashes, impotence, confusion, and, rarely, hepatitis, a drop in the white blood cell count (which can lead to serious infections), increased blood pressure, and heart arrhythmias.[5]

Unless there's some very good reason for you to take a cyclic antidepressant, I would suggest you use a different kind. Talk to your doctor about it. It may mean paying more, but the extra money you spend on a safer drug is likely to be a very good investment in your health.

The MAOIs

MAOIs (monoamine oxidase inhibitors) are used less frequently than the other types. Nardil (phenelzine) is an example of an older MAOI, and Aurorix (moclobemide) is one of the newer ones. Monoamine oxidase is an enzyme found in the human body. In your brain, its job is to break down neurotransmitters like serotonin and norepinephrine. Therefore, decreasing this enzyme's action raises the levels of your neurotransmitters, causing a mood-elevating effect.

MAOIs are considered to be particularly effective for so-called atypical depression—that is, depression with symptoms of overeating, oversleeping, and anxiety. The common side effects of MAOIs are: postural hypotension, weight gain, swollen ankles, impotence or other loss of sexual functioning, and insomnia. MAOIs may also cause dangerous elevations of blood pressure if the person eats foods containing the amino acid tyramine. As a result, people taking these drugs need to be on a restricted diet. They have to avoid alcohol, fava beans, many types of cheese, liver, and a long list of other foods (see Appendix 6 for more details). MAOIs also interact with many medications. If you're a careful person, and are willing to put up with all of these restrictions, MAOIs are not a bad choice, since they're usually pretty well tolerated.

Desyrel

Desyrel (trazodone) is a newer antidepressant and is already quite commonly used in the United States. It causes drowsiness, so many doctors prescribe it as a sleeping aid for depressed people. Since Prozac causes insomnia in many people, Desyrel is sometimes used along with it. Apart from drowsiness, it causes dizziness, headache, low blood pressure, dry mouth, and upset stomach. In rare cases, it causes a prolonged erection in men. This can severely damage the penis and lead to impotence.

Wellbutrin

Wellbutrin (bupropion) is a unique antidepressant that is similar to amphetamine (speed) in its chemical structure. Although it was initially withdrawn from use because it caused seizures in some patients, it seems to be safe for most people. It doesn't affect your heart like many other antidepressants do, so it is good for treating depression in people with heart problems. Like amphetamines, though, it commonly causes insomnia, restlessness, irritability, and headache.

Effexor

Effexor (venlafaxine) is very similar to a natural antidepressant chemical found in chocolate, called phenylethylamine. Effexor's main advantage is that it is said to work faster than other antidepressants. Side effect–wise, a whopping 37 percent of patients report that it makes them feel nauseous, and around 20 percent say it makes them feel drowsy, dizzy, or dry in the mouth.[6] The most serious side effect is an increase in blood pressure, so if you already have high blood pressure, this is not the drug for you.

CHAPTER 11

✦

HERBAL MEDICINE

He preferred to know the power of herbs and their
value for curing purposes, and, heedless of glory,
to exercise that quiet art.
—VIRGIL, c. 30 B.C.E.

St. John's Wort: Nature's Own Prozac

THE Greek philosopher Aristotle believed that all learning consists of rediscovering what we already know in the depths of our minds. Although he wasn't thinking of St. John's wort when he wrote this, his insight describes the story of this remarkable herb very well.

Used for over two thousand years by herbalists in Europe and Asia, modern science has only recently "rediscovered" its healing powers. Through good-quality studies, we now know that St. John's wort is as effective as conventional medication for the treatment of mild to moderate depression. It also has only a fraction of the side effects of conventional drugs. What's more, it is also much cheaper. All things considered, St. John's wort makes our modern synthetic drugs look pretty unimpressive. But traditional herbalists have known about it all along.

St. John's wort, also called *Hypericum perforatum*, Klamath weed, goat weed, as well as many other names (it is said to be the rose of Sharon, mentioned in the Bible's Song of Songs), is one of the most widespread plants in the world. It grows at roadsides and in fields all over Europe, Asia, the Middle East, South Africa, North and South America, and even Australia. It grows in the form of a small bush, only a foot or two tall usually, with woody stems and bright green, spade-shaped leaves. Its golden yellow flowers blossom in late June, around the time of St. John's day in Germany, thus giving it its common name. (Wort is Middle English for plant.)

Early healers were probably inspired to experiment with it because of the blood red oil that exudes from its buds and leaves when they're crushed. According to an ancient healing tradition, plants were thought to contain clues in their physical appearance as to conditions for which they were beneficial. The red oil of St. John's wort, therefore, led to its use for healing deep wounds and infections. Interestingly, modern research has revealed immunity-enhancing and antiviral activities in St. John's wort extracts, validating many of its traditional uses.[1]

Herbalists also discovered its mood-elevating effects, and for centuries, it has been a favorite remedy for depression. Current research has demonstrated that it works as an antidepressant in several different ways simultaneously, with synergistic effects on the brain and the immune system, as I'll discuss below.

Effective and Safe: The Proof

More than thirty controlled studies, including a total of several thousand patients' results, have demonstrated St. John's wort's effectiveness and safety in depression.[2] Even the conservative *British Medical Journal* published an article on it, and commented that "clinical trials suggest that hypericum [St. John's wort] might become an important tool for the management of depressive disorders."[3] In fact, its antidepressant effects might even be slightly *better* than those of imipramine.[4]

These were not merely placebo-induced effects: These trials were double-blind and placebo-controlled, meaning that neither the doctors nor the patients knew whether they were using St. John's wort, standard antidepressants, or inactive placebos. The researchers ensured that the tablets all looked the same, and kept the identity of each of the tablets to themselves. St. John's wort consistently produced outstanding results.

Doctors who are used to prescribing synthetic drugs know that the more effective a drug is, the more side effects it usually has. But this isn't the case with St. John's wort. It does not cause drowsiness, nor does it interact with alcohol.[5] It doesn't cause difficulty in concentration, as many antidepressants do; on the contrary, one study showed that it improves information processing by the brain, even in previously normal subjects—thus acting as a type of "smart drug."[6]

St. John's wort is in a class all its own in terms of how gentle it is on the body. According to the largest study to date, in which 3,250 people were treated with this herb, only around 2.4 percent reported any side effects from it. This is an amazing figure when compared with the 30 to 40 percent or more that is typical of standard antidepressants. St. John's wort's reported side effects, apart from being rare, are typically very benign: stomach upset (0.55 percent of patients); allergic reactions, including skin itching and reddening—it makes you sunburn more easily (0.52 percent); tiredness (0.40 percent); anxiety (0.26 percent); dizziness or confusion (0.15 percent); and a variety of other symptoms like dry mouth, tremor, and sleep disturbances, which occurred in less than one case in 1,500.[7] Compare this with the lists of the side effects of standard antidepressants given in the previous chapter. Even so-called low-toxicity drugs like Prozac have many times the number of side effects of St. John's wort.

Why Doctors Are Still Ignoring Herbs

In my opinion, these findings about St. John's wort are going to revolutionize the medical treatment of mild to moderate depression. In Germany, this has already happened. St. John's wort is a registered medicine there, trusted by family doctors, internists, and psychiatrists. Fifty percent of all prescriptions for antidepressants in Germany are for this remarkable herb. Prozac, in contrast, accounts for just 2 percent.[8]

Still, I think it's going to take some time for St. John's wort to be fully accepted by mainstream medicine outside of German-speaking countries. Despite the impressive research, there's a number of factors in the medical system working against a more widespread acceptance of herbs like St. John's wort.

First of all, most doctors in English-speaking countries are simply ignorant about, and prejudiced against, herbal medications. Although many doctors are curious about them, there's a generalized belief in the profession that herbs are only "pretend" drugs, more likely to do harm than good. This prejudice is supported by an absence of education on herbs that doctors receive in medical school.

Second, a big factor working against herbs is money. Herbs are not patentable. The good thing about this is that anyone can manufacture and sell them, driving down the price. Unfortunately, this also means that it just doesn't make financial sense for drug companies to do research on or market herbs. They can't make enough money out of them.

Researching and marketing medications is very expensive, because the government requires complex and lengthy studies for each new drug. This is intended to protect consumers from unsafe new drugs. But it also means that the drug companies need to get a high return on their products to cover their expenses. The only way they can do this is to patent their drugs so that no one else can produce them. Then they can charge whatever they like for them.

They can't do this with nonpatentable medications like herbs, so they just ignore them. And since drug companies fund most of the world's research on medications, studies on herbs are few and far between. Such studies often receive little or no financial backing.

All of this would not be so bad if doctors were not so dependent on the pharmaceutical industry. Most doctors receive a large proportion of their information about their own profession from drug companies. This occurs either directly—through advertising, seminars, freebies, and so on—or indirectly—by relying on the recommendations of academic specialists, who are frequently in the employ of both drug companies and universities. This information is often extremely biased toward a heavy use of drugs, and generally ignores safer alternatives.

All things considered, it's a wonder that any studies on St. John's wort were done at all! Most of them were conducted in Germany, where the medical profession has an unusually progressive attitude about herbal medications. It is thanks to their open-mindedness that we now have the scientific proof to back up the traditions of the ancient herbalists.

How St. John's Wort Works

As mentioned earlier, no single component of St. John's wort accounts for all of its antidepressant action; instead, several synergistic effects are produced.

Some components of St. John's wort, for example, have been found to cause a change in the number of serotonin receptors on brain cells, much as does Prozac.[9] This Prozac-like effect may well be the main way it works. It also works in a way similar to monoamine oxidase inhibitors (MAOIs) like Parnate and Nardil.[10] This MAOI-like effect, however, is very weak.[11] This is actually a good thing, since MAOI drugs have some annoying side effects, including a capacity to interact with certain foods and drinks, causing high blood pressure. St. John's wort hasn't been found to do that.

Other components of the herb affect the immune system. As I discussed in Chapter 7, in depression, the immune system is out of balance: very high levels of interleukins, which are a type of chemical messenger for the immune system and brain, are produced. Some scientists have argued that this itself leads to all of the symptoms of depression. St. John's wort decreases the production of interleukins, thus helping the immune system work normally again.[12] This immune-regulating effect complements the Prozac-like effect, making the herb an even more powerful antidepressant.

How to Use St. John's Wort

I recommend you use St. John's wort only with the cooperation of your doctor. He should know what you're taking, for your sake, in the unlikely event that anything untoward does happen, like an unusual side effect. Despite my criticisms of doctors, most of them are open-minded people; they are happy to use anything that has been properly demonstrated to work. Show your doctor this book, or give him a photocopy of Appendix 7, For the Health Professional: Review Articles on St. John's Wort. It contains references for articles that review and summarize the dozens of published studies on the use of this herb in depression.

Taking into account both its effectiveness and low number of side effects, St. John's wort performs better than conventional drugs in *mild* depression. At the present time, however, there have been no studies on the use of St. John's wort in severe depression, although some early indications are that it may work just as well for severe cases.[13] But until actual studies have been done on this, we need to play it safe and restrict its use to mild depression.

The best way to take St. John's wort is the liquid extract, available in health-food stores or through alternative physicians. Gel capsules are also available; these are usually less expensive than the liquid extract. Liquid extracts and capsules preserve the active ingredients better than the tablet or raw dried herb forms.

See Appendix 2 for a list of suppliers. Average cost per month for the liquid extract would be in the area of $25 to $30.

The recommended dosage varies among manufacturers, since some extracts are more concentrated. Follow the instructions on the label. Take the extract in water or juice, with meals. Keeping the bottle in the refrigerator is a good idea—it slows down heat- and light-induced degradation.

If you are over sixty-five, start with a low dose—half the normal dose would be reasonable—and increase it only if after four weeks or so you haven't had an adequate effect. People with kidney or liver diseases should only receive St. John's wort (or any medicine) under medical supervision, as should people with high blood pressure. For an extra margin of safety, I recommend that if you have high blood pressure, and your doctor okays your use of St. John's wort, you should follow the same dietary precautions as people on MAOIs (see the previous chapter for details). People with heart failure should avoid this herb. It is also not recommended for pregnant or nursing women, or for children under twelve years of age.

A number of medications, and even some nutritional supplements can potentially interact with St. John's wort, and should not be taken with it. These include all other antidepressant medications; other medications for mental illnesses, like antipsychotics and lithium; diet pills; nasal decongestants; cold or hay fever medications; asthma medications; illicit drugs or narcotics; and the amino acid supplements phenylalanine and tyrosine. Certain asthma medications, like cromolyn sodium, and steroid inhalers, are fine to take with St. John's wort, though you should also check with your doctor.

This is an important point, so I'll restate it: *Do not take St. John's wort if you are currently using another antidepressant.* If your doctor agrees to try you on this herb, you should first cease the other antidepressant under medical supervision, and allow it to fully "wash out" of your system, before starting the St. John's wort.

Like all other antidepressant medications, St. John's wort takes four to six weeks to produce its full effects. Some benefits are usually felt by about the tenth day or so. The first symptoms to improve for most people are the physical ones—insomnia and loss of appetite. Improvement in mood often comes in fits and starts at first, with some good days and some bad.

If you are one of the 2.5 percent of people who react adversely to St. John's wort, you should of course immediately stop taking it and see your doctor.

Recommended Reading

The Natural Prozac Program: How to Use St. John's Wort, the Antidepressant Herb, by Jonathan Zuess, M.D. (New York: Three Rivers Press, 1997), contains interviews with some of the doctors who have done research on the herb, as well as in-depth information on its uses as an antidepressant and antiviral medication. It also looks at the herb's history and traditional uses, and includes a section on how to grow it yourself.

CHAPTER 12

✦

NUTRITIONAL HEALING I: SUPPLEMENTS

I am a little world made cunningly
Of elements . . .
—JOHN DONNE, 1609

The Parable of the Explorer

L ET me take you on a trip deep into a vast, mythical wilderness of stark mountains and gnarled trees. Here, in a deep canyon, staggers an explorer who is lost and has run out of provisions. Suddenly, a wilderness-spirit appears to him and gives him two ways she can help him. The first option is that she could give him some more provisions and a map that will prevent him from getting lost again. The second option is that she could instead place impassable obstacles like tall cliffs and raging rivers all around him, leaving only one narrow, dangerous path that would lead him back home.

If he chose the first option, he would not only arrive home refreshed, but he would also have a map to ensure he did not become lost on future journeys. If he chose the second option, he might still arrive back home—if he survived the route—but he would be hungry and possess no map for the future.

In some ways, a depressed person is like this explorer. I tell this story as a way to illustrate the difference between using supportive natural therapies, like nutritional supplementation, and using drugs. Drugs block the body's processes, forcing them to move along unaccustomed and sometimes perilous routes. As I've mentioned, in major depressive disorder, this is often necessary in order to interrupt the abnormal cycle of the illness. But because this approach fails to empower the bodymind's own healing abilities, it usually isn't the best way to treat people having a depressed response, or a mild case of major depressive disorder. In those cases, drug therapy can result in the weakening of the individual. This is why people who rely solely on drug therapy tend to become ill again when their medication is stopped. These explorers let their innate healing systems go hungry, and are likely to become lost again.

The whole idea of nutritional medicine, on the other hand, is to provide substances to physically nourish the bodymind's own self-healing processes. It involves using substances that would naturally exist in the body anyway, so it is a safer and gentler form of therapy. What's more, optimizing and maintaining a balanced nutritional status strengthens the bodymind for dealing with any future upsets. The explorer arrives home refreshed, and is less likely to become lost again.

Actually, the parable is inaccurate in one important way: There is really a third choice the explorer could pick. He could use both the first and second options at the same time. Nutritional medicine, like most other "alternative" therapies, complements conventional medication very well. If you have a moderate-to-severe case of major depressive disorder, this third choice might be the best one for you. You'll have the map and the provisions, and you'll also have a path laid out before you to give that extra degree of guidance through the roughest terrain.

Just like herbs, nutritional supplements are not patentable, and so they have often been ignored by the powers that be in conventional medicine. But as conventional medicine has become more sophisticated, and more concerned with the prevention of illness, it has slowly begun to accept the importance of nutrition. There is now an exponentially growing database of research on the preventive and healing benefits of vitamins and minerals in many conditions. Depression is no exception.

Powerful, Exciting Results

A number of nutritional supplements have been proven to have mood-elevating effects. Some have been shown to be as effective as conventional antidepressants, but with much less toxicity. Many others have been shown to have less dramatic but still quite real benefits in the treatment of depression. Even conventional medical authorities have recommended that all depressed patients receive certain vitamin supplements. Unfortunately for their patients, most conventional physicians are still unaware of this body of research.

Based on the evidence of their effectiveness, their relative lack of toxicity, and their inexpensiveness, I prescribe vitamin supplements to all my patients with depression as an adjunct to their treatment. I've had good results with them.

Get the Facts, Not the Hype

You are probably already aware that there is a considerable amount of hype pervading the whole area of nutritional supplementation. The health-food industry is a multibillion-dollar concern, and suffers from more than its share of misleading advertising and product labeling. A lot of people are getting ripped off, purchasing products about which misleading claims have been made. And often, even if there is good scientific evidence of a supplement's efficacy, consumers are being sold the wrong dose, or an inferior form of it.

The only way to sort out the wheat from the chaff in this area is to take the time to go through the scientific literature and weigh the evidence for yourself. I've done that for you and present my findings in this chapter. I'll also tell you about possible side effects and contraindications on the use of vitamins and other supplements—information you're not likely to hear from a health-food salesperson. And in Chapter 13, I've included some information on specific dietary alterations aimed at improving mood.

Vitamins and Minerals

DOES OUR DIET REALLY
PROVIDE ENOUGH NUTRIENTS?

We've all heard it, the old homily that "a healthy, balanced diet will provide you with all the vitamins and minerals you need." The homily is actually true—or at least it *might* be if our diet really was healthy and balanced. It might be true if the foods we ate were not grown in mineral-deficient soils, and fed with chemical fertilizers to increase their size at the expense of their nutritional value. It might be true if they weren't picked before ripening to enhance their shelf life, transported and stored for long periods, refined, bleached, overcooked or fried, not to mention coated in herbicides, pesticides, antibiotics, and artificial hormones.

The average person in our society gets the majority of his or her calories from animal fats, and most of the rest from sugar and refined flour. These foods actually create a condition of nutrient-debt in the body. This is because the food has been stripped of most of its vitamins and minerals; yet your body has to use other vitamins and minerals to metabolize them. The average person also has minimal variety in his or her diet—it isn't balanced, and it isn't healthy. All things considered, you're a lucky person if you manage to get through life without a nutritionally deficient diet.

Here's another reason why that homily is only partly true: It's debatable as to what the phrase "all the vitamins and minerals you need" really means. The fact is, the levels of vitamins thought of as "normal" or "adequate" by most authorities—the Recommended Daily Allowances, or RDAs—are only based on how much is needed to prevent a flagrant deficiency disease. The optimal level of that vitamin, meaning the level at which the body's biochemical processes function best, can actually be much higher.

*FACT: VITAMIN DEFICIENCIES ARE
COMMON IN DEPRESSION*

Most conventional doctors believe that vitamin deficiencies are extremely rare in our society. They believe that it's only worth testing for deficiencies in patients who are obviously at risk—those who are malnourished, have chronic gastrointestinal disease, are on a strange diet, or are alcohol dependent.

Clinical psychiatric researchers, however, have been surprised to discover that these beliefs are totally false. They have found that vitamin deficiencies are quite common, and that it is difficult if not impossible to determine whether an individual has a deficiency based on the standard risk factors.

One research group, for example, used blood tests to measure the levels of the vitamins B_1, B_2, and B_6 among psychiatric patients. These patients were mainly middle class and well off. To their amazement, 53 percent were found to be deficient in at least one of these three vitamins. And importantly, they found that vitamin deficiencies had nothing to do with the standard risk factors. The patients didn't have clinical signs of malnutrition, weight loss, or disease.[1]

These results are not at all unusual, and have been replicated many times. For example, another group measured levels of vitamin B_6 in outpatients with depression and found that 20 percent were deficient.[2]

Because of studies like these, conventional psychiatrists have come to consider blood tests for certain vitamin deficiencies to be an essential part of the workup for their depressed patients. A deficiency of nearly any vitamin can give rise to symptoms of depression. Of course, when a vitamin deficiency is found in a depressed person, it doesn't necessarily mean that it *caused* the depression. It may be purely coincidental. Or the depression may have actually caused the vitamin deficiency, by causing loss of appetite and decreased food intake. In some cases, though, studies have shown that a simple vitamin deficiency is in fact the cause of the depression. And in those cases, vitamin therapy is often all that is needed to cure it.

It makes good sense, therefore, for people with depression to routinely take a good-quality multivitamin and mineral supplement.

RECOMMENDED VITAMINS

PLEASE NOTE: The doses recommended below are for adults only. Dosage recommendations are summarized at the end of this chapter.

A deficiency of *thiamin* (vitamin B₁) is sometimes found in people with depression, as mentioned above. You're especially at risk for thiamin deficiency if you abuse alcohol, are on a weight-reducing diet (dieters are at high risk for all vitamin and mineral deficiencies), and drink a lot of coffee or tea. Thiamin is important for many different metabolic pathways, including the conversion of glucose into energy. It also helps protect against lead poisoning—an important function when you consider the heavy environmental lead contamination in many areas today (lead is discussed further in Chapter 14). A severe deficiency of thiamin causes feelings of confusion, visual disturbances, a staggering gait, and decreased sensation in the feet and legs, among other things. Thiamin seems to be quite nontoxic, even in high doses. The recommended dose is from 1.5 to 10 milligrams daily.

Riboflavin (vitamin B₂) deficiency is fairly common in people with depression.[3] Riboflavin is part of the antioxidant defense system of the body. Some signs that might indicate that you have a deficiency are: cracks in the corners of your mouth, or cracked lips, a sore, reddened tongue, and eczema. Using imipramine (Tofranil) or amitriptyline (Elavil) actually makes you more likely to become deficient in riboflavin. So if you're on one of these drugs, you would definitely benefit from supplemental riboflavin, as well as other B vitamins. A recent study has proven this. In this study, patients with depression were divided into two groups: one group took standard antidepressants alone; the other group took supplements of riboflavin, thiamin, and pyridoxine (see below) in addition to their standard antidepressants. The results showed that the group receiving the vitamins felt less depressed and could think more clearly than those taking just the antidepressants.[4]

You're at higher risk for riboflavin deficiency if you're a dieter, if you avoid dairy products (the best natural source of riboflavin), abuse alcohol, or have thyroid disease. Riboflavin is quite nontoxic, and the recommended dose is from 1.7 to 10 milligrams daily.

Deficiency of *niacin* (vitamin B₃) can also cause depression. The full-blown deficiency state is called pellagra, a disease described by "the four-D's": dermatitis, diarrhea, dementia, and depression. The recommended dose is from 13 to 19 milligrams daily. Higher doses—in the order of 100 milligrams daily—can be toxic, causing flushing, stomach upset, and low blood pressure. Doses of over 2 grams daily can cause serious liver damage. Orthomolecular physicians (doctors who specialize in prescribing nutrients), however, often use high doses of niacin in patients with mental illness, along with other mega-vitamin therapies. These patients need to have regular blood tests to check their liver function.

If you have peptic ulcer disease, gout, liver disease, or serious heart-rhythm abnormalities, you should take supplementary niacin only under a doctor's supervision.

Pyridoxine (vitamin B₆) deficiency is common in depression, found in 20 percent of cases, as noted above.[5] Here are some ways to tell if you are deficient: poor immunity, or areas of numbness, tingling, or electric shock sensations in your hands or elsewhere in your body. If you use oral contraceptive pills, you are especially at risk, because your liver uses up a lot of pyridoxine when it metabolizes the pills.

Pyridoxine is involved in the production of brain neurotransmitters and is essential for every organ system. The recommended dose is from 2 to 50 milligrams daily. It can cause serious nerve damage if taken in high doses, so do not exceed a dose of 50 milligrams daily. Unfortunately, a lot of manufacturers market it in high-dose tablets, over 50 milligrams each—this may be unsafe. Check the label.

Cobalamin (vitamin B_{12}) deficiency is a classic cause of depression. All patients with depression should have a blood test to determine their B_{12} status. The only good natural sources of B_{12} are meats, fish, eggs, and dairy products, so if you are a vegan, you should take B_{12} supplements. Despite manufacturers' claims, soy products, yeasts, spirulina, mushrooms, and such contain little or no B_{12}. Deficiency can also be caused by a variety of gastrointestinal disorders, like chronic diarrhea. Some symptoms of deficiency are weakness, fatigue, tingling or electric shock sensations, and a sore tongue. Sometimes, the only symptom of deficiency is depression.[6] The recommended dose of B_{12} is from 5 to 50 micrograms daily. If taken orally, it is safe. When very large amounts are injected, it can be toxic.

Folate (or folic acid) deficiency is another important cause of depression, and like B_{12}, every patient should be tested for it. Folate deficiency causes depression by lowering brain levels of serotonin.[7] Multiple studies have shown that between one-third and one-half of people with psychiatric disorders have a folate deficiency, and that it is most commonly associated with depression.[8] In fact, it has even been recommended by a conventional psychiatric authority that every person with depression should receive supplemental folate.[9]

Symptoms of folate deficiency are similar to those of vitamin B_{12} deficiency: weakness, fatigue, irritability, cramps, and, in severe cases, anemia. The recommended dose is 400 micrograms daily. It is nontoxic.

As I mentioned earlier, the optimum level of a vitamin can sometimes actually be much higher than the RDAs. And even though a person might not have a deficiency of a vitamin (according to the conventional definition of deficiency), they can sometimes still benefit from taking supplements. For example, in the case of vitamin B_{12} and folate levels, a recent study showed that patients at the low end of the "normal" range of blood levels of these vitamins had problems in mental functioning that were not present in patients at the high end.[10] None of these patients met the conventional definition of deficiency, and yet some of them could clearly have benefited from extra vitamins. As natural therapists have been saying for decades, the conventional standards of "deficiency" are misleading.

Vitamin C (ascorbic acid) has also been proved to be beneficial in depression in doses higher than the RDA. In one study, depressed patients were given either a large dose—3,000 milligrams—of vitamin C to drink, or a placebo of similar taste and appearance. The patients given vitamin C felt significantly better. The effect lasted only around six hours, though.[11] This was predictable, since vitamin C, above a certain level, rapidly washes out of your system. It needs to be taken in divided doses, two or preferably three times a day, to maintain therapeutic levels in your body.

Vitamin C has a variety of beneficial effects, including the enhancement of immunity and wound healing. The recommended dose varies greatly depending on who you listen to. The RDA is only 60 milligrams a day, but many doctors recommend doses a hundred times that. With high doses, however, gastrointestinal irritation occurs. Vitamin C may also interfere with the absorption of calcium. It's said that high doses can cause kidney stones, too, but this claim has been debated. Doses of less than 2,000 milligrams or so a day seems to be quite safe; I recommend you take around 1,000 milligrams a day. Decrease the dose if you experience diarrhea.

Vitamin C is usually sold in the form of chewable tablets. Because these tablets are usually acidic, they may cause damage to your tooth enamel. To avoid this it may be best to buy the vitamin in the form of calcium ascorbate powder, and take it mixed into a drink. The powder is expensive but highly concentrated—a single teaspoon equals about 4,000 milligrams, so you only take a quarter of a teaspoon a day. If you are taking large doses of vitamin C and then decide to stop taking it, you should do so gradually. Sudden discontinuation of high doses can produce a deficiency state.

Vitamin E (alpha-tocopherol) is also beneficial in treating depression.[12] It is a powerful antioxidant and seems to protect the brain against a variety of diseases.[13] It enhances immunity, as well. For most people, vitamin E is safe in doses under 600 IUs (international units) daily. One of its side effects is that it makes your blood less likely to clot. As a result, you should not take it if you are on a drug that affects blood clotting, like warfarin, or if you have a known vitamin K deficiency (which also affects blood clotting). Vitamin E can also raise blood pressure, so use only a very low dose (e.g., less than 100 IUs) if you have hypertension. In addition, don't take vitamin E at the same time of day that you take oral contraceptives or iron tablets—it can interfere with their absorption.

RECOMMENDED MINERALS

Research shows that deficiencies of minerals are less clearly associated with depression than deficiencies of vitamins. The story of *calcium* in depression, for example, is not very straightforward. Some studies have shown that depressed people have abnormally high amounts of calcium in their blood, but a few studies have found the levels to be normal or low.[14] We do know for certain, though, that very high calcium levels, such as are found in some medical disorders, are definitely associated with depression—in fact, they can *cause* depression. Everyone with depression should have a blood test for their calcium level. Most psychiatrists do this as part of their patients' routine workup.

I don't recommend supplementation of calcium for depressed people. If your blood calcium level is normal, though, the small amounts of calcium found in most multimineral supplements should not be a problem for you. (Supplemental calcium may be beneficial for the treatment of insomnia, as discussed in Chapter 16.)

Magnesium opposes many of the actions of calcium in the body, so it is not surprising that it has been found to be deficient in some patients with depression.[15] Magnesium is involved in the synthesis of brain neurotransmitters, and it also has a relaxing effect on nerves and muscles. A deficiency of magnesium can cause insomnia, loss of appetite, nausea, diarrhea, high blood pressure, abnormal heart rhythm, muscular weakness, and tremors. Most people do not consume enough of this essential mineral, so taking a magnesium supplement is a good idea. I recommend 200 to 400 milligrams daily. Magnesium gluconate, aspartate, or orotate are the best forms, since magnesium oxide and magnesium hydroxide can cause diarrhea. Do not take magnesium if you have kidney disease or if you are taking diuretics or digoxin. In some cases of abnormal heart rhythm, supplemental magnesium is beneficial, but in others it is dangerous. Most conventional doctors will be aware of this, and you should discuss it with them.

There are several other vitamins and minerals that have been claimed to have benefits in depression. *Chromium*, for example, has been recommended.[16] *Selenium* might also be helpful.[17] Deficiencies of *zinc* have been reported to cause depression in rare cases.[18] The literature on these minerals, however, is sparse. This is not to say that they are useless; one characteristic of vitamins and minerals is that they tend to have many broad-ranging effects on different organ systems, since they are a required part of basic cellular metabolic processes. Health-food salespeople tend to hawk them as though each vitamin or mineral had just one special function, like giving you strong healthy nails or stamina. Though they might provide those benefits, they affect your whole body.

TIPS ON TAKING SUPPLEMENTS

To make sure you're getting adequate amounts of all the essential nutrients, I recommend that you take a good all-around multivitamin and mineral combination. The best sort of supplements are those which come in divided daily doses, rather than a single tablet per day. They're more expensive, but they ensure that you have an adequate level of the more rapidly eliminated vitamins, like vitamin C, in your system throughout the day. You can find divided-dose supplements in most health-food stores.

If you're male, or if you have a chronic inflammatory disease like arthritis, you should avoid multivitamin preparations containing iron. Women usually benefit from supplemental iron because of what they lose through menstruation and pregnancy, but many men have excessive levels of iron in their bodies. High levels of iron increase inflammation, speed up the aging process, and can lead to a worsening of heart disease. Iron-free supplements are available at health-food stores.

Side effects are rare with vitamins when taken in the doses I've recommended. Nausea occurs with some people. But this can be reduced by taking the vitamins with a meal, and by not taking them in the morning. Some people are allergic to the fillers used in many vitamin tablets—starch is one—and should use "hypoallergenic" preparations.

One final note on vitamins and minerals: Any substance can be toxic if taken in a high enough dose, even water, and unless you're being treated by a specialist in nutritional medicine, I do not recommend megadose therapy. Among other serious adverse effects, megadoses of vitamins A or D or calcium can actually cause depression.

SUMMARY

Multivitamin and mineral combinations are best taken in the form of divided daily doses, instead of a single tablet per day, including especially:

Supplement	Daily Dose
B_1 (thiamin)	1.5–10 milligrams
B_2 (riboflavin)	1.7–10 milligrams
B_3 (niacin)	13–19 milligrams
B_6 (pyridoxine)	2–50 milligrams
B_{12} (cobalamin)	5–50 micrograms
Folate	400 micrograms
C (ascorbic acid)	250–1,000 milligrams
Magnesium	200–400 milligrams daily

NOTE: Melatonin, which is classified as a hormone, not a nutrient, is discussed in Chapters 15 and 16.

Amino Acid Therapy:
How to Feed Your Brain

HOW AMINO ACIDS WORK

Amino acids are what neurotransmitters are made of. In depression, the supplies of neurotransmitters in your brain are depleted. By supplementing your diet with the right amino acids, your brain can increase its production of neurotransmitters, which results in an improved mood. It makes good sense to support your body's own biochemical processes using natural dietary requirements like amino acids.

DL-phenylalanine (sometimes referred to as DLPA) is an amino acid used in your brain for the synthesis of norepinephrine and other neurotransmitters. Supplementing your diet with it has been proven, in a double-blind controlled study, to be as effective as imipramine, the "gold standard" in antidepressant medications. In this study, forty depressed patients were randomly allocated to receive either 150–200 milligrams of DL-phenylalanine or 150–200 milligrams of imipramine daily. Neither the patients nor the doctors knew who was getting which medication—the researchers kept this secret. At the completion of the thirty-day trial, results were compared, and no difference could be found between the two groups in their improvements—this simple amino acid was as effective as a drug.[19] In another study, sixteen out of twenty depressed patients (80 percent) who were given DL-phenylalanine improved significantly; eight of them reported complete recovery within three weeks, and eight reported a mild to moderate effect.[20]

The "D" and the "L" refer to different forms of the molecule, whether it is bent to the right or to the left; DL-phenylalanine is thus a mixture of the two forms. In general, our bodies prefer to use only "L" forms of amino acids, which occur naturally in many of our foods. It is this form of phenylalanine that is responsible for most of the antidepressant effect of the DL mixture. In one study using L-phenylalanine on its own, thirty-one out of forty depressed patients (almost 78 percent) benefited from it, and ten of these were reported to be completely relieved of their depression.[21] D-phenylalanine, however, can enhance this effect. It has been shown to help alleviate pain and is thought to work by slowing the breakdown of opiatelike (painkilling) substances in the brain called enkephalins. It may also have antidepressant effects, though studies have reported conflicting results.[22] Combining the "D" and "L" forms seems to be the most effective approach—and this may minimize side effects as well.

I particularly recommend DL-phenylalanine therapy to depressed people who also suffer from some sort of chronic pain (except migraines); for example, low back pain, arthritis, or irritable bowel syndrome. It is also useful for patients who have problems with low blood pressure. These people often cannot tolerate conventional antidepressant medications, because they tend to cause a further drop in blood pressure. Amino acids like DL-phenylalanine may help to raise their blood pressure slightly.

SIDE EFFECTS

DL-phenylalanine does have a number of side effects. There have been a few reports of it causing a dangerously elevated blood pressure. It also interacts with the antidepressant drugs known as monoamine oxidase inhibitors (MAOIs), causing elevated blood pressure when mixed. Phenylalanine in any form (i.e., D-, L-, or DL-) as well as tyrosine (see below) should therefore not be taken by people with high blood pressure or anyone taking an MAOI drug or St. John's wort. In addition, people who have the rare inherited disease phenylketonuria (PKU), or who have had melanoma in the past or currently, should not take them. I also advise against their use during pregnancy. In addition, I am cautious about prescribing amino acids along with any other antidepressant medication, though I know physicians who do this regularly without any ill effects.

If you suffer panic attacks, you should also probably avoid taking supplemental amino acids. These supplements will increase your brain's stores of norepinephrine. Norepinephrine is released during panic attacks, so the increased stores caused by amino acids can make the attacks more intense. Anxious patients tend to report some worsening of their anxiety early on in their amino acid treatment. I should add here, though, that I've seen this problem more often when people are started on Prozac or Zoloft.

An additional side effect of amino acids is that they may provoke migraine headaches in some migraine sufferers. According to the literature, this is a rare side effect, but I have encountered it in one case.

HOW TO USE AMINO ACIDS

Amino acids should probably be used as antidepressants only under medical supervision. You are unlikely to have any side effects, but they should be carefully watched for. All this scary stuff having been said, you should know that amino acids are far safer than conventional antidepressant drugs. And by using the "DL" mixture, it is also less likely that there will be a problem.

The recommended dose of DL-phenylalanine varies from 150 to 1,500 milligrams daily. It is reasonable to start with one tablet daily (they usually come in either 375 or 500 mg. tablets) and if results are insufficient after two weeks or so, to increase the dose gradually up to 1,500 milligrams. Take it first thing in the morning, on an empty stomach. With it, take 20 to 30 milligrams of vitamin B$_6$ (a B-complex vitamin supplement usually contains this), and a piece of fruit or a glass of fruit juice. B$_6$ enhances the effect of phenylalanine; the fruit will help ensure the tablets don't get stuck in your esophagus, and they also help in their absorption. (PLEASE NOTE: Do not take more than 50 mg. of vitamin B$_6$ daily—high doses can cause nerve damage.)

L-*tyrosine* is another amino acid, similar in its effects to phenylalanine. Clinical observations and small placebo-controlled studies suggest that it may be an effective antidepressant, although full-scale studies have not yet been done.[23] In one placebo-controlled trial it was found that supplemental L-tyrosine improved the ability of depressed patients to feel a sense of enjoyment from their daily activities—a significant therapeutic benefit. It was thought that this benefit arose because L-tyrosine increases brain levels of norepinephrine, the neurotransmitter involved in coupling mental or physical activities with the brain's reward mechanism.[24]

It is reasonable to use L-tyrosine in addition to DL-phenylalanine, using similar doses, and if necessary working up to 1,500 milligrams daily. Its contraindications and side effects are the same as for phenylalanine.

AMINO ACIDS TO AVOID

L-*tryptophan* is an amino acid that your brain uses to make serotonin. It has been proven to have benefits in depression, sleep disorders, and chronic pain.[25] It was in widespread use until 1989, when, tragically, a batch of L-tryptophan apparently became contaminated with an impurity, and a massive outbreak of a severe illness called eosinophilia-myalgia syndrome was linked to its use. Twenty-eight deaths were recorded. Even though this was apparently due to an impurity and not to the L-tryptophan itself, I still do not recommend the use of this amino acid until it has been thoroughly proven to be safe.

A number of other amino acids, including *methionine* and *gamma-aminobutyric acid* (GABA), are sometimes recommended for depression in alternative medical circles. In the case of methionine, I know of no studies that demonstrate it to be of benefit. There are a number of good studies on the use of its active form—S-adenosylmethionine—in depression, but unfortunately this substance is not widely available at present.[26] As regards GABA, the literature is similarly sparse. Because it is a calming, or inhibitory, neurotransmitter, it makes sense that high doses could potentially *cause* depression, so at present I don't recommend it. There are bound to be further advances in the research on amino acids, however, and I look forward to them.

SUMMARY

Amino acids—see text for important contraindications

DL-phenylalanine	150–1,500 milligrams daily
L-tyrosine	150–1,500 milligrams daily

The Therapeutic Oils:
Balancing the Essentials

The Kabbalists say that the world rests on the balance between the qualities of loving-kindness and strict justice. The balance needs to be slightly in the favor of loving-kindness, though, or else the harshness of strict justice would destroy the world.

The prostaglandin system is like that. Prostaglandins—the body's regulators—are a group of molecules made out of dietary fatty acids. One group of prostaglandins causes blood vessels to constrict, blood to clot, and pain and inflammation to increase. These are the *2-series prostaglandins*. The other group of prostaglandins opposes all of these actions—keeping blood vessels open and blood flowing, and decreasing pain and inflammation. These are the *1-* and *3-series prostaglandins*. For our bodies to function, we require both opposing groups of prostaglandins, but we need the balance to be slightly in the favor of the 1- and 3-series. Otherwise, we develop diseases involving inflammation, pain, abnormal blood flow, and poor immunity. Imbalances in the prostaglandins have been linked to allergies, menstrual pain, arthritis, angina, cancer, and, you guessed it, depression.

Back in the 1980s it was discovered that the levels of the "bad" 2-series prostaglandins were sky-high in depressed people.[27] Making the imbalance worse, levels of the "good" 1-series were found to be low.[28] This is probably why there are so many immune system problems found in depression, like allergies and recurrent infections, as I discussed earlier. The imbalance is so marked that scientists have even proposed that an accurate way to diagnose depression would be to test for abnormal prostaglandin levels in patients' saliva.[29]

Why do so many of us have imbalanced prostaglandins? The answer has a lot to do with our diets, specifically with our high intake of saturated and trans-fatty acids. Both of these unhealthy fats block the enzyme needed to make the "good" 1- and 3-series prostaglandins. (For further information on what these fats do, and how you can avoid them, see the next chapter.) Alcohol also blocks this enzyme, as do deficiencies of B-vitamins and zinc.

Now for the good news. You can bring your prostaglandin levels back into balance by eating a healthy diet (see the next chapter) and by using therapeutic oil supplements: evening primrose, flax, and fish oils.

These oils have powerful effects on the prostaglandin system. Unfortunately, if they are not used with caution, they can have powerful side effects, too. You should also be aware that although they are widely prescribed by holistic physicians, there are as yet no double-blind studies of their use in adults with major depressive disorder. As a result of this, they should be considered experimental medications. I have not personally prescribed them for patients with depression because of the lack of good studies. I'll discuss them here, however, because many other doctors have claimed success with them, and I think it's likely that in the near future, research will prove them to be correct.

EVENING PRIMROSE OIL

Evening primrose oil contains gamma-linolenic acid, which the body uses to make 1-series prostaglandins (one of the "good" guys). One small placebo-controlled study found that evening primrose oil was helpful in treating depression and hyperactivity in children.[30] Another study found that a combination of evening primrose and fish oils was effective in improving the symptoms of depression in patients suffering from chronic fatigue syndrome.[31] There are also isolated reports that this combination of oils is effective in patients with severe depression.[32]

Evening primrose oil, however, has some side effects. It can worsen temporal lobe epilepsy and trigger mania in people with bipolar disorder (manic-depression).

FLAX OIL

The oil of flax seed (also called linseed) contains around 50 percent alpha-linolenic acid. This is the essential fatty acid the body needs to manufacture the 3-series prostaglandins (the other "good" guys). The typical Western diet is deficient in alpha-linolenic acid. The theory behind its use in depression is sound, but again, there are no studies to guide us. It seems to be fairly safe to use, however.

Flax oil is best purchased in cold-pressed form, packaged in dark bottles, found in the refrigerated section of your health-food store. Check the use-by date, as it's important that it be fresh. If it tastes bitter, it may be too old. The dose is one to two tablespoons per day. Use it on salads, on bread or baked potatoes in place of butter, steamed vegies, or mix it into oatmeal, pasta, or yogurt—*but don't cook with it.* High temperatures damage the oil. If you don't like the taste, try this alternative way of using it: Absorb it through your skin overnight by rubbing it on before you go to sleep and covering the area with a cloth.

Hemp oil is similar to flax oil, containing slightly more alpha-linolenic acid, although it's more expensive. Both oils are considered to be effective remedies for dry skin. You'll need to take them for at least a month before you notice their effects.

FISH OILS

Fish oils (eicosopentaenoic and docosahexaenoic acids) can be used by the body to make the "good" 3-series prostaglandins. In fact, they are only one metabolic step away from *being* 3-series prostaglandins. Flax oil, in contrast, is three steps away. This means that fish oils aren't affected by the metabolic blockers that can stop flax oil from working—like saturated and trans-fatty acids. So if you can't bear to give up french fries or margarine, fish oils could be a more effective way than flax oil for you to raise your "good" 3-series prostaglandins.

The best way for you to get fish oils is in the natural form: Salmon, herring, sardines, bluefish, and tuna are excellent sources. If you don't like fish, there are many brands of fish oil supplements available. Note that cod liver oil is not the same thing, and is not appropriate for this use. It contains high levels of vitamins A and D, which could lead to toxicity if taken in large doses.

The recommended dose of fish oil is from 2 to 4 grams per day. A single 7-ounce serving of salmon will provide this. To retain freshness, store your oils in the refrigerator. Do not use fish oil supplements if you have diabetes or a blood-clotting problem, or are on drugs affecting blood clotting (e.g., warfarin). Use only a very low dose if you have high blood pressure.

Finally, if you are using any form of therapeutic oil, you should also take 200 to 600 IUs of vitamin E daily. This will help protect you from any oxidized fatty acids that might be in the oils.

In summary, you can safely take advantage of the therapeutic oils by adding extra servings of fish to your diet, and using flax oil in your salad dressings and instead of butter. The food you eat can be your best medicine. In the next chapter, I'll discuss other ways to use food for healing.

CHAPTER 13

✦

NUTRITIONAL HEALING II: FOOD AS MEDICINE

Better pay the cook than the doctor.
—*IRISH PROVERB*

What Kind of Diet Is Right for You?

IF there's one thing that's for certain in the field of nutrition, it's that there is always going to be another fad diet coming along, announcing itself as a "breakthrough," claiming to cure just about every disease, and to help you lose weight, too. And more often than not, it seems, this year's dietary guidelines are the opposite of last year's, which were the opposite of the year before. You cannot help but be skeptical of the whole area of diet and nutrition—and even want to ignore it, as do a lot of doctors. And hey, I like brownies, ice cream, and pizza, too, so it's going to take some pretty compelling evidence to persuade me to give them up.

Fortunately, there are a few simple, commonsense measures that have stood the test of time, and can be recommended for just about everyone. I'll lay them out for you in this chapter. We also know that each human being is unique. And in recent years there has been a growing awareness of the concept of individuality of nutritional needs. In other words, apart from a few basic points, a single diet cannot be prescribed that will suit everyone.

Some people are healthiest on a high-carbohydrate diet, while others do better with more protein. Many people also have real problems with particular foods—for example, milk, wheat, sugar, or alcohol. Allergies aren't the only possible problem, either: Some people have hereditary digestive or metabolic enzyme deficiencies, hormonal problems with food, or other factors that make them intolerant of certain foods. As a result, finding the right diet can be a process of trial and error. As I go through the basics, then, I'll also discuss some points that will help you decide what kind of diet is right for you.

The Sugar/Depression Link

Your sweet tooth might be giving you the blues. Patients have often told me about how they'd been "living on sugar" when they were feeling down. Research shows a very strong link between sugar and depression. Several studies, for instance, have shown that when you remove sugar from your diet, your feelings of depression improve, and so do other symptoms, like anxiety and fatigue.[1] Cutting down on sugar can also improve your immune functioning, allergies, and reactive hypoglycemia (see below).

Why should something as seemingly innocuous as sugar have such a strong effect on mood? To answer this question, I'll first explain the difference between simple carbohydrates, like sugar, and the healthier complex carbohydrates.

Complex carbohydrates are the type that occur naturally in grains, vegetables, and so on, and are what your body is designed to use as its main energy source. You digest and absorb them slowly, thus providing your body with a steady supply of blood sugar over many hours.

Simple carbohydrates, on the other hand—such as sucrose, glucose, and honey—are rapidly absorbed, causing intense blood sugar peaks. High blood sugar levels in themselves cause subtle damage to proteins throughout your body, disrupt metabolic processes, and depress your immune system. High blood sugar levels can also cause your metabolism to go into panic mode, overreleasing insulin in an attempt to bring the levels back down. Then, when too much insulin is released, your blood sugar level drops too low (reactive hypoglycemia). This makes you feel fatigued, weak, shaky, hungry, and, sometimes, depressed. Since your blood sugar is low, you crave more sugar, and attempt to get rid of your symptoms rapidly with another simple sugar "fix." This sets up a vicious cycle.

Carbohydrate Craving

As you can see, it's no coincidence that when you're depressed, you often crave simple carbohydrates like sugar. Part of the reason for this is the way depression is linked to reactive hypoglycemia. There's another link between sugar and mood, though, involving the serotonin system. After you eat carbohydrates, your brain briefly increases its production of serotonin. In depression, your brain is starved of serotonin, and craves anything that will boost serotonin levels. Eating carbohydrate-rich food therefore becomes a form of short-term self-medication.[2] For some people, it becomes a way of stuffing down their feelings. If they feel upset, they eat sugary foods to keep the bad feelings at bay for a little while.

If you find that you tend to crave carbohydrates, there are two other things you should know. It has been discovered that the effectiveness of a carbohydrate meal in increasing brain serotonin has nothing to do with its sweetness. A bread roll, for example, works as well if not better than a candy bar.[3] So keep some healthy complex carbos around rather than reaching for the junk food. Complex carbos will give you the same serotonin boost without causing the vicious cycle of reactive hypoglycemia.

The other thing you should know is that light therapy has been found to be particularly effective for depressed people who crave carbohydrates. (This is discussed in Chapter 15.)

What all this information leads up to is a basic nutritional point for everyone: Choose complex carbohydrates over simple ones—that means grains, legumes, seeds, nuts, vegetables, and other natural foods—rather than foods with a lot of sugar and refined flour in them. I also strongly recommend that you eat wholemeal products in preference to refined ones, and organically grown produce where possible. Whole, organic foods contain a maximum of nutrients and fiber, and a minimum of toxins.

How Much Carbohydrate Is Best?

Okay, we've determined that a diet based on sweet stuff is not a good idea, and that complex carbos are the way to go. Nothing new there. But how much complex carbohydrate should you eat: Should it be the basis of your diet, as most nutritionists recommend, or should it be minimized, as one of the recent dietary fads would have you do? You may have already heard about diets like the "Zone diet," which recommend a lower carbohydrate intake with a higher percentage of fat and protein.

The theory behind the low-carbohydrate diets seem to make sense. It goes like this: All carbohydrates, whether simple or complex, cause an elevation of insulin levels in the body. Insulin, though important for regulating blood sugar, also encourages the production of the "bad," inflammation-promoting compounds, 2-series prostaglandins. An excess of these compounds, as I mentioned in the previous chapter, is associated with a host of diseases, including depression. To avoid all of this, say the promoters of the diet, you should keep your carbohydrate intake low, and instead be sure to eat a higher percentage of protein and fat with every meal. It is claimed that this will help boost your mood (and help you lose weight, prevent disease, etc.).

The problem that I have with their diet is this: Good-quality studies have shown that people eating a diet precisely *opposite* to what they recommend have more vigor and significantly fewer feelings of depression and hostility than other people. In other words, research shows that a low-protein, low-fat, high-complex carbohydrate diet is best.[4] This means a mainly vegetarian diet, low in sugar.

What's more, you simply do not need to go on a low-carbohydrate diet to reduce your levels of "bad" 2-series prostaglandins. You can do this more easily by supplementing your diet with flax or fish oils, as discussed in the previous chapter.

Nonetheless, there is no doubt that some people will feel better with fewer carbohydrates. For example, some people are intolerant of virtually all grains; suffering from severe gas, loose stools, eczema, or any of a wide variety of subtle allergic reactions whenever they eat them. Also, some people with reactive hypoglycemia do best on a high protein and fat diet.

Personal experimentation is the key here. If, after a few weeks of eating one way, you don't start to feel better, try changing the proportions of carbos, fats, and proteins around. You can keep eating the same kinds of foods you usually do, just eat less of some and more of others. For example, if you normally eat spaghetti with meatballs, try leaving out the meatballs. Or if you normally eat mainly carbos, try adding more protein-rich foods, for example, an extra serving of tuna or cottage cheese. And remember, when you try out a new diet, don't expect changes overnight. Dietary changes usually take at least six weeks to show results.

Why You Can Stop Worrying About Cholesterol

For most people, I recommend they eat a mainly vegetarian diet, with the inclusion of fish and, very occasionally, meat. This brings up another issue about food and mood that's been in the media eye lately: cholesterol. Some psychiatric researchers believe that many of us are not eating enough of it. That's right. Several recent studies have shown that very low levels of blood cholesterol are associated with depression and suicide.[5] Does this mean we shouldn't be vegetarians, that we should all eat more cholesterol-rich animal products?

In a word, no. First of all, the data on cholesterol and depression is conflicting. A large study in 1994, for example, found that there was no evidence that low cholesterol levels could cause or worsen mood disorders.[6] Studies in 1995 and 1996 confirmed this.[7] In fact, some of the best available data has shown that people who ate a healthy diet to lower their cholesterol actually had improvements in their mood.[8] Furthermore, those studies that claimed low cholesterol caused depression weren't clear on whether the depression was a side effect of the cholesterol-lowering drugs or of using unhealthy weight-loss diets. So it's unclear whether our cholesterol levels have much to do with our moods at all.

Because everyone is unique in their biochemical makeup, however, I still think it's likely that there are *some* people who'll be happiest and healthiest with a moderately high blood cholesterol level. Yet even in their cases, it doesn't follow that they would need to eat more cholesterol-rich animal products. The reason for this is simple: Most of the cholesterol in our blood is actually manufactured by our livers. Only a small percentage of it comes from diet.

Why do our livers produce cholesterol? Cholesterol has many essential functions in the body. It is made into hormones. It is a prime ingredient of cell membranes. It also protects cell membranes from damage due to unhealthy dietary fats like saturated fatty acids (found mainly in animal products and processed vegetable oils) and trans-fatty acids. Trans-fatty acids are toxic forms of fat that are produced by heating or oxidation of fats.

Processed or synthetic fats, like margarine or shortening, contain a lot of trans-fatty acids. So do natural fats that have been damaged by high temperatures, as in frying or broiling, or by prolonged exposure to air or light. That's why fresh, natural cold-pressed oils are better for you. The term *saturated fatty acid* means that the fat molecule has lots of hydrogen atoms attached to it (in other words, it is fully *hydrogenated*). This makes the fat more solid and sticky, more like shortening than oil. Unfortunately, this stickiness means that both saturated and trans-fatty acids tend to get stuck in cell membranes, clogging them—damaging the delicate membranes and making them prone to inflammation. This is a major cause of atherosclerosis. These toxic fatty acids also encourage the formation of the "bad" 2-series prostaglandins—and hence they are linked to depression.

Cholesterol is the body's antidote to the membrane damage caused by saturated or trans-fatty acids. It inserts itself into the membranes, making them less sticky again. So if you eat a lot of these toxic fatty acids, your liver will manufacture more cholesterol to protect you from them. (But if too much cholesterol is inserted into the membranes, this also causes damage, promoting atherosclerosis.)

Clearly, if we just avoided saturated and trans-fatty acids in the first place, we wouldn't have to worry about cholesterol. You can do this by avoiding animal products and synthetic oils, including all types of margarine and shortening.

Manufacturers of snacks and prepared baked goods like cookies and cakes have made this a difficult task. They use hydrogenated oils and shortening in just about everything to give their product the right texture. Fortunately, if you read labels, you'll discover that there are one or two brands of most products that are free of these toxic oils. If you can't find them in your grocery store, try a health-food store. Or if all else fails, you can always bake your own.

The Truth About Synthetic Fats

Despite what the advertisers of margarine claim, there is no such thing as a synthetic fat that is good for you. Besides containing unnatural trans-fatty acids, margarine, shortening, and other synthetic fats have another big problem: They consist of only a few varieties of fatty acid molecules. Oils that occur in nature contain mixtures of many different molecular types, and so our livers contain a variety of different enzymes to metabolize them. An onslaught of just a few types of molecules, such as is found in synthetic products like margarine, effectively floods the corresponding enzymes in the liver. This overwhelms the body's ability to metabolize them. The excess unmetabolized fat molecules overflow into the circulation, causing damage to the lining of blood vessels throughout the body.

In addition, it's a little known fact that polyunsaturated fatty acids—the main type of fatty acid used in margarines—are powerful immunosuppressants. In high doses, for example, they are sometimes used to prevent graft rejection in patients with kidney transplants.[9] There are also concerns that they may be carcinogenic in humans, as they are in animals.[10]

Cold-pressed virgin or extra-virgin olive oil is high in monounsaturates and is the healthiest cooking oil you can purchase (actually, it's just the *least unhealthy*). Canola oil ranks second in cooking oils. I recommend that you go through your kitchen and toss all the others into the garbage. But please: Do not dispose of oils down the drain—they damage our waterways. And yes, butter is better for you than margarine, but it's still not actually *good* for you, so use it sparingly. For salad dressings and other nonheated uses, the best oils are flax and hemp, as I mentioned earlier.

Chocolate: Why It's Good for You

No discussion of dietary fats would be complete without reference to the sovereign of all foods: chocolate. This stuff is surprising. True, it's high in fat, but cocoa butter in itself is not really that bad for you as far as fats go. Chocolate also contains compounds called phenylethylamines, which are chemically related to the neurotransmitters that occur naturally in our brains and are thought to have antidepressant effects.[11] In addition, chocolate is high in healthy magnesium. On the down side, it contains caffeine, which is unhealthy (see Chapter 8), and is usually mixed with a lot of sugar and milk fat. And some people are allergic to it. So it's a mixed bag. I think that as long as you're not troubled by insomnia (caffeine makes it worse), and you stick with good-quality dark chocolates—avoiding milk chocolate, compounded chocolates, or chocolates with oils or a lot of sugar added—you should be fine. Enjoy!

I want to make one thing clear before I leave the subject of dietary fats: In general, I am against dieting with the intention to lose weight. In many cases it causes more problems than it solves, and in fact can predispose you to depression. If you eat the diet I recommend—mostly vegetarian, low in sugar—and you exercise regularly, your body will find the weight that it functions best at all by itself. Naturally, this may be higher or lower than the latest fad body shape. Despite the antifat bias of the medical profession, people can be fit and healthy if they're overweight. Eating a healthy diet is entirely a different thing to dieting with the aim of losing weight.

Protein: Will I Get Enough?

One thing that people who are starting to eat a mainly vegetarian diet worry about is getting enough protein. But even people who are 100 percent vegetarian get ample amounts of protein— from whole grains, rice, corn, beans, and so on. (Strict vegetarians like these, however, need to take supplemental vitamin B_{12} and iron.)

Most people in our society consume far too much protein, especially protein of animal origin. They mistakenly assume that we require it. In fact, a single four-ounce serving of protein-rich food a day is more than adequate to meet your body's need for protein; most people eat that much at every meal. Your body must get rid of the excess, and it is just burned as fuel. Unfortunately, proteins are much more difficult to burn (metabolize) than carbohydrate or most fats. They also leave behind a nitrogenous residue that must be processed by the liver and excreted in the urine, a process that places strain on these organs and can be the cause of a persistent state of low-level fatigue. People complaining of fatigue will sometimes experience relief by simply reducing their protein consumption.

High-protein, high-meat diets have another problem: When meat is heated to very high temperatures, as in frying or broiling, compounds called heterocyclic amines are produced. These compounds are toxic to nerve cells and disrupt the production of neurotransmitters, thus opening a predisposition to depression. (Food coloring is another source of heterocyclic amines; see Appendix 5 for a list of these. The most concentrated sources of heterocyclic amines are cigarette smoke and petroleum fumes.)[12]

As if all this wasn't enough, high-protein diets also leach calcium out of your bones and contribute to osteoporosis. Plus, they worsen allergies—a point with special relevance to people with depression, as I'll discuss below.

Do You Have an Allergy?

Clinical ecologists have long claimed that food allergies play a role in some cases of depression, but the topic remains controversial. They have some good evidence on their side. Allergy and depression are very strongly linked statistically. An unusually high proportion of people with depression have a history of allergies (hay fever, eczema, hives, asthma, etc.).[13] Both conditions are also known to involve similar biochemical imbalances (low norepinephrine and high acetylcholine levels), but in different areas of the body—depression in the brain, allergies in the autonomic nervous system. According to some researchers, allergic reactions can therefore accentuate the chemical imbalance in the brains of depressed people.[14]

Interestingly, people with allergies who are depressed have a different emotional profile from other depressed people. They are characterized by their increased emotional sensitivity. Because of this, researchers have suggested that allergic reactions are really only just one manifestation of an overall tendency toward excessive sensitivity—both on the physical and the emotional levels.[15]

The association between allergy and depression has been well proven, but whether food allergies *cause* depression is another question altogether. There is some evidence that they can. A placebo-controlled double-blind experiment found that in some individuals, psychological symptoms—including severe depression—could be produced by exposure to allergens placed in the mouth.[16] Furthermore, there have been many anecdotal reports by doctors of their success in treating depression by removal of allergens from the diet.[17] In some patients, the improvement has been dramatic. I've found that the benefits are usually more modest and tend to be mainly in generalized symptoms like fatigue and irritability.

If you are interested, it is worth trying to eliminate milk and all milk products, the commonest food allergens, for a period of eight weeks. Replace them with soya substitutes, and be sure to take your multivitamin supplement so you get enough riboflavin. Other common allergens include wheat and eggs. A formal elimination (or antiallergy) diet is the best means of discovering any food allergies you may have, but it can be something of a major undertaking. Many allergy therapists recommend restricting your diet very severely, and this can be stressful in itself. Because of this, I have included guidelines for a much simpler, low-stress, antiallergy diet in Appendix 4.

An alternative to the elimination diet is fasting for a period of about four days. Where there are multiple food allergies, sensitivity to one food often increases sensitivity to another, which in turn increases sensitivity to another, and so on, setting up a vicious cycle. A period of total abstinence from food can break this cycle of sensitivity, and after the fast you may find that you no longer react to previous allergens. PLEASE NOTE: Fasting is dangerous for many individuals, can cause serious mood upsets, and should not be undertaken without medical supervision. I do not recommend you try it if you currently have major depressive disorder.

If you are interested in pursuing the treatment of food allergies further, a doctor who specializes in allergies or environmental medicine (i.e., clinical ecology), or a naturopath, would be the best person to help you. I would also refer you to your local library, which will probably have books on the topic of food allergies.

Low-Vanadium Diet

There is another specific type of dietary modification that has been demonstrated to have benefits in depression. Over the last decade, research has been published showing that patients had dramatic improvements in their depression when eating a diet low in vanadium, especially when they were also given supplemental vitamin C.[18] Vanadium is a mineral in our diet that appears to be nonessential, though we don't know for certain. In several studies, vanadium levels have been found to be two to five times higher in depressed people than in other people.[19] It appears that it may be toxic, and that it may be a cause of manic-depression.[20]

What kind of diet do you eat to avoid vanadium? Surprise! It's the same diet I've been recommending all along—mainly vegetarian. Fruits and vegetables have the lowest amounts of vanadium in them. Meat, seafoods, and dairy products contain a slightly greater amount of vanadium, and so should not be eaten frequently. You should also avoid black pepper and dill, since these are the richest sources of vanadium.

Eating to Save the World

I've discussed a few of the reasons to eat a mainly vegetarian diet already. There are many more. Ethics and ecology are two of them. If you're eating vegetarian, you are not contributing to the suffering of animals, and you are making a far more efficient use of the earth's resources than if you ate meat. (It takes ten pounds of grain to produce one pound of beef.) You are also not contributing to the destruction of the rainforests to make way for cattle grazing land. Aren't those reasons in themselves antidepressants?

Traditional cultures ground all their practices, including the details of their diets, in their religions or belief systems. They recognize the deep interconnectedness of all things. In contrast, our society tends to fragment everything. We treat nutrition and ethics as if they were somehow independent of each other. I believe that it's wrong to separate them.

Everything in Moderation

Inscribed on the stones of the ancient Greek temple of Delphi were the words: *Nothing to excess.* I've discussed a lot of different dietary modifications for the improvement of your mood in this chapter, but I wanted to conclude it on this note. Plenty of people have been caught up in diet extremism, and that on its own can have a negative influence on mood and overall health. Like the world itself, human beings are sustained only by balance. Optimum nutrition comes from eating in a balanced way, which means allowing yourself to have a variety of different natural foods.

When you think about it, the phrase "everything in moderation" means being moderate even in your moderation. In other words, it's okay, even healthy, to occasionally have an excess of some things. A dietary lapse is not a sin. And if you don't like the diet you're eating, change it! Be gentle on yourself, and enjoy your eating.

Some Good Cookbooks

Hot and Spicy and Meatless, by Dave DeWitt, Mary Jane Wilan, and Melissa T. Stock (Rocklin, Calif.: Prima Publishing, 1994), contains spicy vegetarian recipes from around the world, including Two-Chile Quesadilla Ecstasy, Habanero Lasagna, Avocado Feta Frittata, and Spicy Pandang Fruit Salad. This is an excellent cookbook, though I recommend you use less oil than the recipes call for. You can also pan-steam or microwave vegetables instead of frying them.

Feast for Health, by Colin Spencer (London: Dorling Kindersley, 1987), is a sensible, well-balanced approach to nutrition with simple but very classy recipes.

The Natural Healing Cookbook, by Mark Bricklin and Sharon Claessens (Emmaus, Pa.: Rodale Press, 1981), contains 450 good recipes from the editors of *Prevention* magazine, with a discussion of the best foods for specific health problems, including anxiety and depression. Some of its nutritional information is out of date, but it is still an excellent book.

Jane Brody's Good Food Cookbook (New York: Bantam, 1987) is a good resource for low-protein, high-carbohydrate nutrition.

Transition to Vegetarianism, by Rudolph Ballantine, M.D. (Honesdale, Pa.: Himalayan International Institute, 1987), is a favorite cookbook among naturopaths, aimed at helping reduce the amount of animal protein in your diet.

Summary

Diet—mainly vegetarian, with plenty of fresh (preferably organic) fruits and vegetables, whole grains, legumes, beans, and so forth. Have fish regularly, and meat occasionally. Avoid sugar, food colorings, black pepper, and dill. Check labels and avoid anything "hydrogenated" or "partially hydrogenated," or any kind of shortening. Replace your oils and margarine with cold-pressed olive oil and use it sparingly. Try flax oil in your salad dressing.

CHAPTER 14

✦

ECOLOGY AND DEPRESSION

We need the tonic of wildness . . . We can never
have enough of nature.—HENRY DAVID THOREAU

. . . the whole problem of health in soil, plant, animal
and man is one great subject.—SIR ALBERT HOWARD

Healing Earth

WHEN my patients discuss the things they feel have led to their depression, they can usually identify many interacting factors. I've noticed that one of the most common factors they mention, especially the younger patients, is the degradation of our global environment.

I have to agree with them—it is an extremely distressing topic. I also know that a positive use can be made of that distress. It can motivate us to change our lifestyle to become more environmentally friendly. We can reduce, reuse, and recycle. We can plant native vegetation, use public transportation or bicycles, avoid phosphate-based detergents, use our own cloth bags to carry our groceries, compost our organic garbage, eat vegetarian, join an environmental lobbying group like the Sierra Club, and so on. There are literally thousands of things you can do to improve the environment, and every one of them makes a real difference.

The things that are good for the earth are also good for you. Vegetarianism and bicycling, for example, are environmentally friendly options that will also improve your health and your mood. This is no accident. We evolved as part of the biosphere of this planet, to live in harmony with it. In recent decades we have come to understand that we cannot fully separate our own health from the overall health of the planet.

Because we are integral parts of our planet, environmental degradation distresses us not only psychologically but physically as well. There are numerous pollutants that affect our health, and some that are clearly linked with the development of depression. This is true not only for chemical pollutants but also to a lesser extent for electromagnetic radiation and noise pollution. In this chapter I'll discuss how you can work out if you've been affected by these factors, and what you can do about it if you have.

Lead Toxicity

It's been estimated by the National Institute for Occupational Safety and Health that over 800,000 American workers are exposed to high concentrations of lead daily, and that 10 to 20 percent of them have abnormally high levels of lead in their blood.[1] Lead is still used in some glazes, as well as in pipes, sheet metal, and foils, but most lead poisoning these days occurs in people working outside of those areas traditionally considered to be at high risk. Dust from building demolition and fumes from gasoline (though leaded fuel is banned in most areas now) are common sources.[2] In urban areas throughout the world, levels of general environmental contamination with lead—soil, water, and air—are high.

Early symptoms of lead poisoning include fatigue, irritability, depressed mood, insomnia, nervousness, headache, and weakness. In 1984, the *American Journal of Psychiatry* published a report of four men diagnosed with severe depression who were found to have low-level lead poisoning. Remarkably, their depression was cured when they received treatment for the lead poisoning. The authors emphasized that the classic symptoms of lead poisoning—abdominal pain and loss of sensation in the hands and feet—may not necessarily be present, and that psychiatrists should suspect lead poisoning as a cause for depression more often than they do.[3]

I know of a case of a man who had been hospitalized in a psychiatric institution for years before an observant doctor noticed that he was slightly anemic, and that he had a dark line on his gums near the teeth—both rare signs of lead poisoning. Chelation therapy cured him, and he went home to live a normal life again.

I recommend that you have a test for the level of lead in your blood if: you reside in an area of heavy lead contamination (e.g., inner-city areas or areas with heavy industry, especially smelting) or have in the past resided in such an area, worked as a painter or in building demolition or metalwork, or worked in a job with high exposure to gas fumes or car exhausts (gas pump attendants, parking garage personnel, etc.). The best person to consult with would be a specialist in the area of either occupational medicine or environmental medicine, since most other doctors would have little or no experience with lead poisoning.

Lead poisoning is treated by removal from the source and the administration of medications called chelators, which bind lead and other metals and allow them to be excreted through the urine. Until recently, this had to be done in a hospital or clinic, since chelating drugs could only be given intravenously, but they are now available orally (e.g., DMSA) and can be used by patients at home.[4]

Naturopaths, who do not have access to these drugs, use high-potency multimineral and vitamin supplements, as well as sulfur-containing amino acids, and a diet high in fiber and sulfur-containing foods, including garlic, onions, beans, oat bran, pectin, and psyllium seed husks.[5] This approach is gentler and less expensive, but also less effective.

There are a number of ways you can reduce your exposure to lead, apart from avoiding high-risk jobs.

- If you are stripping or burning old paint (lead paint was banned in 1978), use a good-quality gas mask, even when outdoors.
- Purchase purified drinking water or, if you can afford it, a water purifier; the reverse-osmosis type is very good and is becoming more affordable (under $200). Less expensive carbon-based filters also remove lead quite well. Purified drinking water is especially important if you live in an area with very old water pipes, which may have been soldered with lead. Some manufacturers of water faucets are still using lead washers in their products, though most have agreed to cease this practice by 1999.
- Wipe the tops of your wine bottles with a vinegar-soaked paper towel before you pour—the metal foil may contain lead.
- Avoid buying imported canned food, as in some countries tin cans are sealed with lead.
- A few patent medicines imported from China contain heavy metals, including lead. American practitioners of traditional Chinese medicine are concerned about this and prefer to personally mix their own herbal formulas, or use the new American-made products.

Several do-it-yourself kits are now available to test for lead in water, dust, soil, paint, or ceramic glazings and cost under $20 or so. They are available in department and discount stores. For more information on lead-related health issues, you can call the National Lead Information Center Hotline on 1-800-LEAD-FYI.

Mercury Toxicity

Can your dental fillings make you depressed? A few years ago, a number of articles were published about the alleged effects of mercury amalgam fillings (silver dental fillings) on mood states and immunity. Some people claimed that they had recovered from depression, chronic fatigue syndrome, autoimmune diseases, and so on after replacing their amalgam with nonamalgam fillings. But does this really make sense?

Most dentists say it doesn't. Establishment dental organizations pooh-poohed these articles, and threatened to deregister dentists who removed amalgam fillings. However, the controversy hasn't gone away. In fact, as research into this area continues, it's getting harder and harder to dismiss.

Doctors actually knew, as early as the nineteenth century, that mercury poisoning causes feelings of anger and depression. These symptoms occurred commonly in hat makers who used mercury in their craft (this is the origin of the term *mad hatters*).[6] Nonetheless, it was controversial whether amalgam fillings released enough mercury to cause any toxic effects.

There is now good evidence from postmortem studies, though, that there is a direct correlation between the number of amalgam fillings a person has and the level of mercury in the brain.[7] And another study showed that when compared to people without amalgam fillings, those with them have higher levels of fatigue, insomnia, anger, anxiety, and depression.[8] A problem with that last study, however, is that it failed to determine whether people with amalgams were angry and depressed merely because they had heard about the negative effects of amalgams, or whether they were angry and depressed as a direct toxic effect of the mercury in their brains.

In other words, the evidence against amalgam fillings is now stronger, but it is still circumstantial. Replacing your fillings can be a costly and painful project, too, so I would only recommend it if other treatments were inadequate for you, and/or if you were well off enough to easily afford it. I do recommend to all patients that any *new* fillings you receive should be nonamalgam ones.

Dentists still prefer to use amalgam because, being 50 percent mercury, amalgam fillings are soft enough to continue to mold to the shape of the cavity over time. Nonamalgam fillings are stiff; if the tooth gradually decays away beneath one, the fillings do not have the ability to mold to the new contour; instead, they tend to crack and fall out. Advancements in materials technology, however, are starting to overcome the inadequacies of nonamalgam fillings.

Apart from its use in amalgam fillings, mercury remains widely used in industry and as an agricultural fungicide. The treatment for mercury poisoning is the same as for lead.

Other Poisonous Metals

Other common metals, including copper and aluminum, are also capable of inducing depression in high doses. If there are blue-green stains where the water drips into your sink or tub, or a bluish tinge to your water, you probably have old, corroded copper water pipes. If you've been drinking that water for years, you may have an overload of copper in your body. You should purchase a water purifier for your drinking water.

As for aluminum, most people are already aware of the dangers involved with chronic ingestion. It is suspected of contributing to Alzheimer's disease, though the issue remains controversial. To err on the side of safety, I agree with the commonly cited recommendations against using aluminum cookware and aluminum-containing antacids.

Chemical Solvents

If you do a lot of work with paints, cleaning agents, glues, or other compounds containing chemical solvents, you may also be at risk for depression. The effects of solvents on the brain increase with increased exposure, and even low-level exposures can be significant if they occur over a long period.[9] Apart from depression, other common symptoms of chronic low-level exposure include absentmindedness, confusion, and dizziness.[10] If you are exposed to solvents on the job, it would be worth your while to discuss them with a specialist in occupational medicine. Write down the names of the solvents, glues, dyes, or other chemicals you're exposed to and show the list to the specialist. He or she will help you to work out which, if any, could be responsible for your symptoms, and how to reduce your exposure to them.

In general, if you are in any doubt about a chemical, avoid it if at all possible. In most cases of solvent poisoning, there is no effective treatment other than stopping the exposure from occurring. Alcohol amplifies the toxic effects of solvents on the brain.[11] If you work with solvents and are unable to avoid them, you should avoid drinking alcohol.

Electromagnetic Radiation

We are profoundly sensitive to the energy fields around us. Electric and magnetic fields are known to decrease the pineal gland's secretion of the mood-regulating substances melatonin and serotonin. Some studies have now shown that there is a link between depression and living next to high-voltage power lines.[12] Other studies, however, have found no link, so the effect is quite probably a weak one.[13]

After much uncertainty, it has also recently been discovered that electromagnetic fields have a weak influence in the causation of leukemia and brain cancer.[14] Because of this, I have no hesitation in recommending that, if possible, you should move if you are currently living next to high-voltage power lines or large electrical installations. Smaller neighborhood power lines are not likely to be a problem.

Magnetic fields grow exponentially stronger as you move closer to them, so even small sources can be dangerous if they are placed right next to your body. Try to avoid being near electrical appliances while they're in use, especially powerful ones like washing machines and heaters. Blow dryers, electric can openers, cordless and cellular phones emit strong fields as well. Clock radios, televisions, and other electrically powered items should probably be placed at least ten feet away from your bed. I also recommend that you throw away your electric blankets. Battery-powered clocks do not produce a strong enough field to have much of an effect, so it's probably safe for them to be near the bed. It also makes sense to arrange your furniture so that your bed and any chairs that you spend a lot of time in are well away from the area where the main power line connects to your house.

Noise Pollution

We are really just beginning to understand the effects that noise pollution has on our health. It has an impact on sleep and mental performance, and recent studies show that in some people, it intensifies physical symptoms, anxiety, and depression.[15] It may just be that some people are more sensitive than others. But our ears are not designed to cope with the high levels of noise many of us are exposed to from vehicles, machinery, loud televisions, and music—noise-induced deafness and ringing in the ears (tinnitus) are becoming more common, even in young people.

Most noise in urban areas is from traffic. If you are unable to move to a quieter location, you can protect yourself to some degree by building fences, or better yet, by planting thick barrier shrubs. If you work or sleep in a noisy area, put up thick curtains, and invest in some ear plugs. If you are able to, avoid using earphones.

The Natural World

At the gates of the forest . . . we find Nature to be the
circumstance which dwarfs every other circumstance. . . .
These enchantments are medicinal, they sober and
heal us.—RALPH WALDO EMERSON

Living in an urban environment, it is easy to lose touch with the processes of nature. The ebb and flow, senescence and renewal, that constitute the earth's rhythms are an important part of who we are, too. They support us, and the truth is that we are totally enmeshed in them. For example, though we control much of the food chain and may feel above it all, we really remain utterly dependent on it. Our society at times severs us from the source of our own life forces. I believe that this sort of alienation from the natural world places us at risk emotionally; through the loss of a sense of groundedness and belonging in the world.

There is now scientific evidence to support this belief. Researchers in the fields of clinical psychology and environmental design have recently published data showing that contact with nature, even as little as a walk among trees or a view of trees out a window, improves mental functioning and overall coping abilities in people who are ill or under stress.[16]

From the earliest days of city-dwelling, people seemed to have sensed this. Cities of the ancient world had gardens where their citizens would relax. Today, most of us have some sort of garden or plants that we tend, as well as animals to keep us company. These things are extremely important. It's also a good idea to go out several times a year—through the changing seasons—to where wild things grow and live. This can prevent you from losing your perspective; it is also a way to renew your spirit.

CHAPTER 15

✦

LIGHT

Truly the light is sweet, and a pleasant thing it is for the eyes to behold the sun.—ECCLESIASTES 11:7

The sky is the daily bread of the eyes.
—RALPH WALDO EMERSON

Margaret's Story

MARGARET learned the hard way about light. An experienced intensive care nurse at forty-one years of age, she had had her first episode of major depressive disorder when she was working the night shift ten years ago. She remembers that experience well. The first thing she had noticed was that everything in her job seemed to be getting harder and taking longer to do. Her mind felt fuzzy, and she made more and more little mistakes, like forgetting to sign medication orders or change bedsheets. She would have to double-check everything to make sure she'd done it properly.

She had initially put this down to simple tiredness— although she was sleeping heavily through the day. But then she became aware of an inexplicable darkness of mood that settled over her. She felt annoyed and morose all of the time, snapping at her husband and workmates for minor things. She started to gain weight, despite the fact that she didn't seem to enjoy eating anymore. And she felt no energy left to do anything other than drag herself through her chores.

Her family doctor diagnosed her with depression and started her on an antidepressant. He also advised her to take a vacation.

She did this, and improved rapidly when she got back on a daytime schedule.

The following year, in the late winter, it all started to happen again—despite her staying on the day shift. This time her depression took months to lift. From that year on, every few years, she would have another episode of depression during the winter. One episode was severe enough for her to require admission to a psychiatric hospital, which was where I first met her.

At the time, she was living in a small apartment that was dimly lit with bluish fluorescent bulbs and had no windows on the sunny side. As I went over her history with her, the seasonal pattern of her illness, and its relationship to light, became obvious to both of us.

I advised her to spend an hour each morning sitting in the sun in the hospital's garden. She did this, and improved more rapidly than she had ever done before. She was discharged a week later, and found that she remained well as long as she spent a half hour to an hour outside on winter and spring mornings.

What she really needed, like many of us, was sunshine in her life.

Sunrays, Seasons, and Body Clocks

Light is essential for human well-being. Without good-quality light—best in the form of full-spectrum, naturally occurring sunlight—many people become depressed. When they are reilluminated, their mood lifts.

In fact, bright light is considered by psychiatrists to be the treatment of choice for a type of depression called seasonal affective disorder (SAD). In SAD, there is a regular relationship between the onset of an episode of mood disturbance and a particular time of year. It usually occurs in winter, but it can start up in any season. Light therapy is very effective for lifting depression in SAD, and it works even more rapidly than medication. Light has also been scientifically demonstrated to be effective in non-seasonal types of depression, although there aren't enough studies in this area yet, and it remains controversial.[1]

The reality is that there is a lot of overlap between SAD and other types of depression. In practice, I've found that many of my patients who have had recurrent depression have some sort of seasonal pattern to their illness. Often, like Margaret, they themselves do not recognize the pattern until it's pointed out to them. For these reasons, and also because it is a safe, simple, natural, and life-enhancing form of treatment, I believe light therapy should be recommended to all people who are depressed.

How and why does it work? There has been some fascinating research into these questions over the past decade. It's thought that light exposure affects your brain's circadian rhythms, providing a sort of reset mechanism for the proper timing of biological cycles.

The secretion of many different hormones in your brain and the rest of your body follows a rhythmical daily cycle. The pacemakers controlling these rhythms are believed to be groups of cells clustered along the nerve pathway from the retinas of your eyes to your pineal gland, and within the pineal gland itself. The pineal is a pea-size gland that is located in the center of your brain. It functions as a sort of biological clock, setting the pace for daily circadian rhythms and also acting as a timer for longer cycles—for example, timing of the onset of puberty. It secretes many hormones, including melatonin, which brings on sleep and increases serotonin levels in your brain. When your retinas are exposed to light, they produce nerve impulses that travel directly to your pineal gland, and reset its rhythmical secretions.

The Third Eye Really Exists

The story of the pineal gland is fascinating and little known, so I'll digress and discuss it briefly. In most vertebrates, the pineal gland is directly sensitive to light, receiving light through an area of very thin bone on the top of the skull. In reptiles, for example, it acts as a third eye (biologists call it the parietal eye), enabling the reptile to navigate by the sun. It is also sensitive to magnetic fields, and probably acts as a kind of compass. In humans, the pineal gland is also sensitive to magnetic fields, and its secretion of melatonin can be upset by exposure to such fields—for example, by those produced by electrical power lines.[2] This is probably the reason why living next to high-voltage power lines is a risk factor for depression, as discussed earlier.

It's interesting to note that the human pineal gland retains its functions as a sensor for light and magnetic fields. It is, in a real sense, our third eye—orienting us in space by sensing our position in the earth's magnetic field and, in time, by sensing the changes in light and darkness. René Descartes, the seventeenth-century French philosopher, believed that the pineal gland was the organ through which the insubstantial spiritual essence, or soul, interacted with the body. Eastern spiritual traditions also tell us that we all have a "third eye" located roughly in the center of our heads, which can be opened through meditation, enabling us to see into spiritual realms. Modern science, on the other hand, tells us that our pineal "eye" looks not into some insubstantial, "higher" spiritual realm but into the physical world of time and space. Perhaps this is because this world is, in many senses, a spiritual realm . . . but I digress. . . .

In any case, your pineal gland and the other rhythmically secreting areas in your brain and body can have their functioning disturbed by altered environmental light levels—both too dim during the day, or too bright during the night. Stress, late nights, exposure to electromagnetic fields, loud noise and vibrations, poor nutrition, and even strong smells can disrupt your pineal's rhythm.[3]

If your pineal's cycle of melatonin secretion is disturbed, you're likely to end up with insomnia, and your brain serotonin levels drop. Disturbances of melatonin and serotonin secretion also alter your mood, appetite, and many other functions of your brain, giving rise to the symptoms of depression. Other cyclical hormone systems can in turn be upset, like that of cortisol, one of the major regulators of your body's metabolic and immunological activities. If cortisol's rhythmical secretion is disturbed, your whole body can begin to function sluggishly.

One of the beauties of the system, though, is that it can be reset quite simply, by regular exposure to bright light in the mornings.

How to Light Up Your Life

I recommend early-morning exposure to bright light for around an hour a day. Go outside in the morning and walk around the neighborhood. Watch the clouds, sit in the sun, do some gardening. Cloudy days are fine, unless the clouds are very thick. In general, however, there is a direct dose-response relationship with light: The brighter the light, the better the effect.[4] But you should of course avoid looking directly at the sun—it can permanently damage your eyes.

If the light is not good enough in the morning, go out at any other time of day. Even though one hour of morning light therapy is considered to be the standard, evidence suggests that other times in the day are just as effective, and as little as fifteen minutes may do it.[5]

In most areas there are enough days with sufficient light in the sky to provide a good effect, even in the winter. If not, you may need to purchase a set of high-intensity, full-spectrum fluorescent lights for indoor light therapy. Standard lightbulbs are less effective—it seems that for a maximum response, the light should be very bright, and preferably full-spectrum, to imitate natural sunlight.

Bright-light units are now marketed by a number of different companies around the United States. They are available either as units that sit on a tabletop or as a visor that projects light directly into the eyes. A device that produces a gradual increase in the intensity of light, called a dawn simulator, is also available. It can be used to wake you in the morning—a sort of light-alarm clock. It appears to offer all the benefits of real sunshine.[6] (See Appendix 3 for information on where to purchase these products.) They are expensive, but your health insurance might cover some of the cost. PLEASE NOTE: Tanning lights are not suitable for this sort of light therapy, since they're designed to produce a high proportion of UV radiation.

Most studies to date have been conducted using bright-light units. With these units, the dose of light is more easily standardized for research purposes, and its indoor administration is more comfortable in the winter than going outside for sunlight. But since the high-intensity, full-spectrum light the units produce is essentially intended to reproduce natural sunlight, why spend a lot of money on an imitation when the real thing is free? Being outside in the real sunlight has additional benefits, including exercise and fresh air, so that's what I usually recommend.

If you don't want to go outside, an acceptable alternative to artificial light in winter might be the use of a sunroom. It should have large windows and/or skylights facing the sun, and white walls to maximize reflection.

Research has shown that you can predict who will respond especially well to light therapy. If you have a tendency to crave sweets late in the day, for instance, you are likely to benefit from it. If you oversleep, rather than undersleep, you are also more likely to have a good response.[7] And certainly, if you have a clear-cut seasonal pattern to your mood, it's very important for you to have light therapy.

Side effects of light therapy are mild. Ultraviolet-related skin or eye damage is the main one. The therapeutic effect comes through light's effects on the visual system, not the skin, so if you're using sunlight or non-UV-shielded full-spectrum fluorescent lights, it makes sense to cover up, and use a high SPF sunscreen on your skin. This is especially the case if you are taking MAOI-type antidepressant medication (including phenelzine and tranylcypromine) or the herb St. John's wort, since these have a photosensitizing effect—that is, they make you sunburn easily. And don't wear sunglasses—that would nullify the effects of the light therapy.

If you're using full-spectrum fluorescent lights, you might also experience headaches or eyestrain as a result of the treatment. If this occurs you should decrease the time you spend exposed to the light. Light therapy is so effective that it can lift some people's mood too high—into a state of pathologically elevated mood called hypomania. A feeling of being "wired," overactive, or irritable might be experienced. If this occurs you should cease the therapy and see your doctor.

In summary, light therapy is proven to be highly effective and is one of the safest treatments for depression that exists. I consider it to be an important part of the overall holistic treatment plan for people with depression.

Are Tinted Glasses a Risk for Depression?

If we need regular exposure to full-spectrum light to keep us healthy, what effect might tinted glasses, which block out part of the spectrum of light, have on us? It would be reasonable to predict that they would put us at risk for disrupted biological cycles and depression.

There has been no research into this question as yet. So what I'm going to say here is only based on anecdotal observations. I've noticed that there seems to be an unusually high percentage of patients with depression and other low-serotonin conditions (like chronic pain syndromes) who wear tinted glasses. It's not only myself who has noticed this: I also once gave a talk about chronic pain syndromes to a group of orthopedic surgeons, and one of them commented, out of the blue (no pun intended), that he'd noticed that many patients with such syndromes wore tinted glasses.

Obviously, tinted glasses don't cause depression in everyone who wears them. But they may be a risk factor. I'd recommend that if you do have problems with depression, you should have your tinted lenses replaced with nontinted ones. If you wear sunglasses occasionally, such as for driving, that should be okay. But if you're wearing tinted glasses all day, you are starving yourself of natural light. The same is probably true if you have tinted windows throughout your home and workplace.

Melatonin Supplements for Depression

If light works as an antidepressant by resetting your pineal gland's production of melatonin, will taking melatonin supplements have the same effect? There's a lot of interest in this question these days, but so far we don't know the answer. The problem with using melatonin supplements in depression is that it is not as natural a way to reset your body clock as sunlight is. Instead of allowing your body to respond naturally to its intended environmental signal (sunlight), melatonin supplements override this response.

That's why it doesn't surprise me that in the studies that have been conducted so far, melatonin supplements haven't been found to be as effective an antidepressant as light.[8] Granted, these studies haven't been conclusive. In one of them, the researchers gave the melatonin at the wrong time—during the day, not at night, basically turning the natural cycle of melatonin upside down. That could hardly have been expected to reset the melatonin cycle properly.

I believe a properly timed melatonin supplementation (i.e., a sustained-release preparation given at night) might eventually be found to help at least a subgroup of depressed people. At present, though, using it for depression would have to be regarded as purely experimental.

We do know that as a sleeping aid, melatonin is very effective. In the next chapter, I'll discuss how to use it. I'll also tell you about many other natural, nonaddictive ways to improve your sleep.

CHAPTER 16

SLEEP

Oh sleep! It is a gentle thing,
Beloved from pole to pole!
To Mary Queen the praise be given!
She sent the gentle sleep from heaven
That slid into my soul.
—SAMUEL TAYLOR COLERIDGE

A Primal Mystery

SLEEP is a wonder and a mystery. Not simply a period of physical rest, it is in fact a period of great activity, especially of your brain and endocrine systems. Complex, poorly understood functions are switched on and off at specific intervals. Your bodymind processes the activities it has undergone during the previous day, both physical and emotional.

The process of falling asleep is also more complicated than you might think. It's not just a cessation of normal daytime activities; it actually requires the switching on of special sleep functions. It is a skilled activity of your bodymind. Like other skills, it can be forgotten—leading to insomnia—but it can also be relearned. This chapter contains a scientifically proven program for relearning the skills required for refreshing sleep and increased daytime energy.

Interestingly, it is not really known for certain why we sleep. Regeneration and renewal processes can go on at any time; we don't necessarily have to be asleep for them to work.

There is some scientific evidence, however, that one of the main reasons we sleep is so we can dream, as I discussed in Chapter 2. Some Eastern mystics claim that sleep is entirely unnecessary, that they never sleep—having "evolved" beyond it—though I am skeptical of this claim. There is no doubt that some people need less sleep than others, particularly older people, but I think that to be completely sleepless would be to miss out on an elementally human physiologico-psycho-spiritual process.

On the other hand, it's easy to get uptight about sleep. Some people get upset, irritable, and tired just by worrying that they're not getting enough sleep. Four or five hours may be all their systems really need, but they believe the messages our society gives that less than seven or eight hours is abnormal.

Sleep and Melancholy

Poor sleep and depression go hand in hand. Some experts even believe that a sleep disorder may be the primary cause of depression. Certainly, disordered sleep can lead to disruptions of melatonin, serotonin, cortisol, and so on, reproducing the patterns found in depression. And trouble sleeping is frequently the first symptom that people experience when they become depressed.

Most people with depression get too little sleep—having difficulty getting to sleep or staying asleep—and some get too much. Classically, difficulty staying asleep (early morning wakening) is said to indicate a worse degree of depression, but many mildly depressed people also have this problem.

Excessive sleep is often a feature of seasonal affective disorder (SAD). Along with the other features of SAD, like carbohydrate cravings, fuzzy-headedness, and depressed mood, it usually responds very well to light therapy, as described in the previous chapter.

How to Sleep Better—A Proven Program

Your insomnia will tend to improve as you move out of the state of depression, as part of the overall program in this book. So it will probably not be necessary to focus treatment specifically on your sleep. But if sleeping is particularly troublesome for you, you'll find below a program of specific steps you can take. Recent research has proven this drug-free program to be effective in the treatment of chronic insomnia. The patients with chronic insomnia who underwent these steps had significant improvements in their sleep, and increased daytime energy levels.[1] You will notice that parts of the program overlap with the treatment of depression, because the two conditions—chronic insomnia and depression—are so similar.

Fixed wake-up times and bedtimes: Find the times that work in your life now and stick to them. This helps reset your body clock. Don't take naps. You can very gradually extend your scheduled sleep time as your insomnia improves. Here's how you might do this: Say you decide to start with a set sleep time from 1:00 A.M. to 6:00 A.M., for a total of five hours a night. Get into bed at 1:00 A.M., and set your alarm for 6:00 A.M. If you find you're sleeping all the way through this period, add fifteen minutes to it the next week. In other words, in your second week, your set sleep time would be from 1:00 A.M. to 6:15 A.M. If you find you're sleeping all the way through this, increase it in the third week to 1:00 A.M. to 6:30 A.M., and so on. But if you find you're not sleeping all the way through your new set sleep time, don't increase it. Keep your set sleep time the same until you find you're sleeping all of the way through. Then, when you are sleeping through it, add fifteen minutes to it the next week, and so on.

If you awaken before your set wake-up time and can't get back to sleep within ten minutes, leave the bedroom and go sit in an

armchair: You may have to spend the rest of the night in the armchair, but the bed is to be your sleeping place, not your lying-awake place. In general, you should also not work or read in the bedroom.

Fixed eating times: This also helps establish your body clock's regularity.

No alcohol: Although alcohol has a sedative effect at first, it actually keeps you awake afterward.

No caffeine after breakfast: Preferably no caffeine at all—this includes coffee, cola, tea, and chocolate. Cigarette smoking should also be ceased, as should any other stimulant you're taking.

Late-afternoon exercise: Take a twenty-minute walk in the late afternoon every day. This raises your body temperature, which will begin to fall later in the day. A falling body temperature is thought to be one of the triggers for sleep.

Early-morning exposure to bright light for forty-five minutes: Quite apart from its ability to lift mood in depression, light treatment has been demonstrated to be one of the most powerful aids to the treatment of insomnia, increasing total sleep time and decreasing the time you need to get to sleep. Bright light is a signal that the brain and endocrine system requires to set its day and night modes properly. (Go back to the previous chapter for more information.)

More Tips for a Good Night's Sleep

- A warm bath after your afternoon walk can help raise your body temperature as well, so that it cools off later and helps you sleep.

- Make your bedroom a sleep haven. A comfortable mattress and pillows; soft, comfortable linens and blankets; adequate heating or cooling; curtains to block out stray light; and a "Do not disturb" sign on the door can all help. Keep your room clean, too. You could also play a cassette tape of the surf or of a heartbeat (available in larger audio stores).
- Learn how to relax. There are many different ways—deep breathing, stretching, meditation, yoga. (See Chapter 17 for more information about relaxation.) You also need to be able to redirect your mind away from your worries as you lie in bed at night. Counting sheep might be too boring, so try visualizing yourself in different sorts of peaceful scenes. You might try imagining yourself driving along a country road in the springtime, or paddling down a gently flowing river. Go over the plot of your favorite book or movie in your mind, or anything else that might relax you.

Melatonin: The Sleep Hormone

Melatonin is a hot topic these days. Studies suggest it has antioxidant, even anticancer, effects, but more definitively, it has been proven to be a potent and safe sleeping aid.[2] As discussed in the last chapter, melatonin is a hormone secreted by the pineal gland. Normally, its blood levels are high at night and low during the day. It brings on feelings of fatigue and drowsiness, and is one of the main triggers for sleep.

Melatonin tablets are currently available without prescription. They can decrease the time you need to get to sleep, and decrease the number of times you wake up at night.[3] And unlike sedative drugs, it doesn't suppress REM sleep, and doesn't produce a hangover.[4] Those are pretty impressive benefits.

Now here's the catch, or rather, the two catches: First, there's evidence that melatonin supplementation is only effective for people who have abnormally low levels of melatonin in the first place, like most elderly people.[5] In other words, it might not work for younger people. Second, we don't know what side effects its long-term use might have. Just because melatonin is a "natural" substance doesn't mean it's risk free. Other natural hormones, like thyroid hormone, estrogen, or corticosteroids, sometimes cause dangerous side effects. Granted, melatonin supplements are in widespread use, and so far, there have only been a few reports of adverse effects. If melatonin is used during daytime, it can cause confusion and fatigue, and possibly worsen depression.[6] High doses might also cause suppression of sexual functions. So, in summary, melatonin needs to be used with caution.

Natural Ways to Raise Your Melatonin Levels

There's a natural way to get all the benefits of melatonin without the risks: maximize your brain's own melatonin production.

Using the nondrug treatment program for insomnia outlined above will raise your melatonin levels without the need for supplementation. There are also a few other things you can do to help this process:

- Use only dim lights after sunset.
- Avoid sources of electromagnetic radiation, especially around your bed (see Chapter 14 for more information).
- Avoid loud or emotionally jarring music after sunset.

If you want to use supplements, remember that they are really still experimental. Use only a low dose—1 milligram or less—and only for short periods (e.g., no more than four days in a row). Taking it for longer periods carries the risk of shutting down the brain's own melatonin production. If you use higher doses, make sure your doctor is aware of it.

Sleeping Tablets and Addiction

Many doctors still treat insomnia with hypnotic drugs such as the benzodiazepines temazepam and oxazepam. These drugs can be addictive. After using them for more than a few nights in a row, your brain stops producing its own natural sleep chemicals, and so your sleeplessness becomes worse if you stop using the drug. The normal cyclical functions of the brain and endocrine system are disrupted, and the result is that your sleep is unnatural and not as refreshing. Sleeping tablets should never be used for more than a few nights in a row. This also goes for all of the various types of over-the-counter sleeping tablets.

Tragically, there are huge numbers of people addicted to sleeping tablets in our society. If you are, talk to your doctor about a detoxification plan—it may be simpler than you think. The usual method is to switch the person over to a longer-acting sedative drug like diazepam, so that the levels of the drug in the body won't vary wildly, causing withdrawal symptoms, and then gradually reduce the dose down to zero over a period of several weeks.

Herbal Sedatives

There are several herbal sleeping aids available. They are not as strong as conventional medications, and thus are also less addictive. They do, however, interfere with your body's natural sleep cycles, and therefore should also not be used for long-term treatment. Two of the better herbal sedatives are valerian and hops.

Extracts of valerian *(Valeriana officianalis)* have been shown in studies to have sedative properties and to improve the quality of sleep in those with insomnia.[7] It is widely used, and is relatively safe. In high doses it can cause nausea, giddiness, blurred vision, restlessness, headache, and grogginess. There has also been a report of liver damage from its use. It interacts with alcohol, antihistamines, other sedatives, antidepressants, and other psychotropic drugs, and you should not use it if you have liver or kidney disease, or are pregnant or lactating, or in children under age five. The most potent way to take it is in the tincture form, available at most health-food shops. Keep the tincture refrigerated. I do not recommend the commonly available tablet form, as the effective ingredients break down when dried, processed, and stored in the tablet form. The dose of tincture will vary according to its strength, so refer to the label. Reduce the dose if you are over sixty-five.

Hops *(Humulus lupulus)* is the ingredient that gives beer its bitter flavor. It is related to marijuana and contains a sedative chemical (2-methyl-3-butene-2-ol) that increases in concentration as the herb dries. Unlike other herbs, then, the best way to take hops is in the form of an infusion of dried, aged leaves. Use two teaspoons of herb per cup of boiling water, and steep for five minutes. It is fairly safe, though rashes have been reported in people handling it. It may cause nausea. It should not be used by pregnant or nursing women, or in children under five years. Reduce the dose if you are over sixty-five.

PLEASE NOTE: I do not recommend the use of these herbs for more than a few days; they should only be used for acute insomnia. They are not part of the overall program for chronic insomnia.

Nutritional Sedatives

Calcium and magnesium are natural neuromuscular relaxants. I recommend taking 1,000 milligrams of calcium and 200–400 milligrams of magnesium half an hour before bedtime. Most grocery stores carry calcium supplements, but you may need to go to a health-food store to find magnesium. Magnesium is available in many different forms, some easier to absorb than others. Chelated magnesium is excellent, as is magnesium gluconate. Other preparations can cause diarrhea. Do not take magnesium if you have severe kidney problems or a high-grade heart block.

With these supplements, try eating a portion of complex carbohydrates, like a slice of bread or a plain baked potato. Carbohydrates increase the production of your brain's own sleep chemicals. Research shows that they have a sedative and relaxing effect in humans.[8]

Excess intake of simple carbohydrates, including raw sugar and honey, can cause reactive hypoglycemia, which is another cause of insomnia. Low blood sugar levels during the night set off the release of epinephrine, and you wake up feeling jittery, hungry, and miserable. To avoid this problem, try eating six small meals a day, low in sugar and refined flour, and high in complex carbohydrates. You might also benefit from a higher intake of fat and protein than most people (see also Chapter 13).[9]

One of the most important messages of this book, and of holistic medicine in general, is that all the parts of our lives are interconnected. As I've discussed elsewhere in this book, one of the results of this interconnectedness is that illnesses such as major depressive disorder or chronic insomnia can sometimes be caused by factors in your life that you might not have thought of, like a poor diet, or a lack of sunshine. Not enough exercise, or too much of it, might also be a big factor. We'll look more closely at this in the next chapter.

CHAPTER 17

✦

MOTION AND RELAXATION

Push on—keep moving.
—THOMAS MORTON, C. 1820

Robert's Story

LOOKING after himself properly was something Robert had never felt he'd had the time to do. In college he'd been an accomplished swimmer, but since joining a large marketing firm, his lifestyle had been taken over by his demanding work schedule. Now he was in his late forties, out of shape, eating a diet of take-out food, and on medication for his blood pressure. He'd gone through a divorce three years ago and since then had been unable to sleep well. When he had tried to discontinue using the sleeping tablets his regular GP had prescribed, he'd been dismayed to discover that he was unable to sleep at all. He'd also felt intermittently depressed since the divorce.

Clearly, Robert's depression was related in large part to unresolved feelings about his divorce, but it was also being contributed to by several other important factors. His sleeping tablets and his medication for hypertension had a depressant effect. So did his diet. And so did his overwork and physical inactivity. Robert was determined to avoid any further medications, and was not interested in psychological approaches, but he was very interested when exercise was recommended as a therapeutic option.

After a thorough physical examination and an electrocardiogram, he began a program of gentle swimming and walking on alternate days. He found that exercise gave him an immediate mood-boosting effect, lasting several hours. This was especially welcome in the mornings, which had previously been his worst time of day. It also helped him to sleep more soundly at night, and he slowly weaned himself off the sleeping tablets without any problems. He decided to reserve the sleeping tablets for the occasional "emergency" night.

Robert also worked on reducing the saturated fats and refined foods in his diet, and increasing his vegetable, whole grains, and fish intake. In addition, he took a number of nutritional supplements including garlic, flax oil, magnesium, coenzyme Q10, and multivitamin and mineral tablets. When starting this program he took two weeks off from work. Once he had gotten into it, though, he found that exercise and good nutrition were easier to fit into his life than he'd imagined, and he was able to continue them while at work, with only minor scheduling adjustments. Within six weeks he was able to reduce the dose of his antihypertensive medication to half of what it had been, with a normal blood pressure, and he was no longer depressed.

He said that he felt exercise acted as a sort of safety net for him. Whenever he felt stressed, or if he felt a dark mood coming on, he would go for a swim or a walk/jog, and this would prevent him from getting any worse. Although some issues regarding his divorce remained, Robert's story is a good example of the way in which a holistic approach brings benefits to your entire being, and is truly restorative of health.

Motion and E-motion

Exercise is a natural antidepressant. Studies consistently show it has mood-elevating effects, in addition to its beneficial influence on every other system of the body. In several studies people even recovered from depression using exercise as their only treatment.[1]

Physiologists have come up with many theories about why exercise is such a strong antidepressant. They talk about increases of blood flow and oxygen to the brain, increased endorphin levels (endorphins are the brain's own "feel good" chemicals), and raised overall levels of neurotransmitters like norepinephrine. Psychologists, on the other hand, believe that exercise works as a general stress coping mechanism, by providing time for yourself, enhanced self-esteem, and so on. They are probably all correct.[2]

I believe the reason it works can be more easily summed up. Physical activity makes us feel better simply because it is what we are designed to do. Humans are made to move. Our bodies thrive, and stay strong and flexible for much longer, if we use our capacity for movement on a regular basis.

The Conscious Body

Exercise is a way of being consciously present in your body. This in itself is restorative. You might spend the whole day involved in the world of thoughts, emotions, or social interactions, but when you exercise, you ground yourself in your physical being again. It is a way of refreshing a vital force that might otherwise become distanced from its roots.

Your exercise does not need to be particularly taxing. Twenty to thirty minutes of aerobic exercise, three times a week, is all you need. If you are feeling really depressed, though, I recommend that you exercise daily.

All types of exercise are suitable. In simple terms, the word *aerobic* basically refers to exercise that works the cardiovascular system—like walking, jogging, T'ai Chi, swimming, or bicycling. Anaerobic exercise, like lifting weights, is also an effective antidepressant. Even very gentle but focused physical activity, such as yoga, has been found to deliver benefits.[3] The best kind of exercise for you is the kind that you enjoy the most, the one you'll be most likely to stick to. A variety of different activities is also good, to prevent boredom.

One of the best ways to exercise is to make it part of your normal daily activities. You can bicycle to work, or walk instead of drive to the shops. That way you avoid having to find extra time for it in your schedule. If you have the time, though, joining a gym or fitness studio is a good idea. A regular class, an enthusiastic instructor, the music, and sharing the exercise experience with others can help overcome the lack of motivation that is a problem for a lot of depressed people. In addition, I recommend that if you are unfit or on medication, you should get a check-up before you begin an exercise program.

If you're exercising outdoors, a particularly good time would be in the morning, to give you the added benefits of morning light therapy. Late afternoon is another good time to exercise, since if you raise your body temperature at this time, it will begin to fall again around bedtime, providing a natural trigger for sleep.

Whatever type of physical activity you choose, an important general rule is that if you find yourself pushing hard, or if you're hurting, slow it down. Overtraining can have negative effects on your mood. The saying "no pain, no gain," is just plain baloney. At the end of your training session you should have plenty of energy left, and not feel exhausted or in pain.

The exercise industry makes a lot of money out of how intimidated people feel about exercise. We think that if we don't have the "right" clothes, the "right" equipment, and so on, we can't exercise right. This, too, is baloney. You can "just do it" without buying their $150 shoes. You should be able to find good-quality running or walking shoes for under $80 or so.

So keep it simple, gentle, and above all, fun!

Relaxing

*Learn to get in touch with the silence within yourself and
know that everything in this life has a purpose.*
—ELISABETH KÜBLER-ROSS

It is essential for you to be able to take your mind off your problems for at least a short period each day. This is something we instinctively seek out in order to create balance in our lives. For example, it's one of the main reasons we have hobbies or other interests, like exercise or gardening. But when you're confronting a serious problem, it can be difficult to focus on other things. Sometimes a specific technique for relaxation can be of help.

There are many types of relaxation exercises. I give one of the simplest and most powerful ones here. The meditation exercises in Chapter 3 are also useful for relaxation.

Progressive Muscle Relaxation

We accumulate a lot of tension and stress in our bodies. Every time we experience excessive stress but don't deal with it consciously, it remains stored in the form of nervous and muscular tension. As time passes, it becomes a constant background feature in our bodies, and we get used to it. We forget what it's like to live in a relaxed body.

Progressive muscle relaxation is an exercise that enables you to experience the difference between tension and relaxation, and so helps to reeducate your nervous and muscular systems. It takes only a few minutes and can be practiced almost anywhere.

To learn this exercise, set aside ten minutes for yourself, and go to a quiet place where you will not be interrupted. You can sit in a chair or lie down.

First, take three deep, slow breaths, focusing on moving your abdomen and then your chest, filling and emptying your lungs with each breath.

Now clench your fists as tightly as you can. As you do so, feel the tension in your hands and arms, and the strength of your muscles contracting. Concentrate on that feeling for a moment, make a mental note of it, and then relax your hands. Let them lie loosely in your lap or by your sides, feel their heaviness, the tension draining away as gravity pulls them down. Concentrate on how they are feeling now, and make a mental note of it.

Now pull your arms in tightly to your chest, clenching the muscles in your arms, chest, and stomach as strongly as you can. Feel the tension, make a mental note of it, and relax. Let your arms lie limply, like a rag doll's, tension draining away. Make a note of that feeling.

Next, clench your feet as tightly as you can, and concentrate on feeling their strength and their tension. Make a note of it, and relax, letting them go limp, tension draining away. Note that feeling of limpness. Repeat this with muscles in your legs, and then your lower back.

Now, shrug your shoulders hard up toward your ears, repeating the same steps of noting the tension, then relaxing, and noting the relaxation.

Wrinkle up your forehead as tightly as you can. Then scrunch up your face—eyelids, lips, cheeks—and repeat the same process.

Next, let your attention wander to all the areas you tensed and relaxed before. If any areas are not relaxed, tense them again. Note the tension, and then relax them, and note the relaxation. It's okay if you need to go through all the areas again.

Finally, feel your entire body in a relaxed state, heavy, all tension drained away.

With this technique, you are teaching your nervous and muscular systems a basic skill: the ability to differentiate between tension and relaxation. You can use it anywhere: at work, when shopping, watching TV, or in bed before falling asleep.

Coping with Difficulties

It's important to remember the true definition of stress: Stress is what you feel in response to a difficult situation; it is not the difficult situation itself. And because stress is actually your response, you can change it.

A certain amount of stress is helpful, because it motivates you to improve your performance—for example, by speeding up your reflexes in a dangerous predicament. However, prolonged or excessive feelings of stress can actually diminish your ability to cope.

The reason you feel excessively anxious or uptight in difficult situations is because you have learned to react that way. You need, instead, to learn to react in a relaxed way. You do this by rehearsing difficult situations in your mind, then applying a relaxation technique like progressive relaxation to calm yourself. As a result, you'll learn how to remain relaxed in the face of troubles.

Stress is a classic body/mind response. The more worried you are, the more physically tense you get, and the more stress hormones your endocrine glands produce. This leads to more anxiety and fear—a vicious cycle that can culminate in a state of full-blown panic. The cycle, however, can be broken at any stage—for example, through reducing your level of physical tension, as in the exercise above or through psychological exercises, such as those I'll discuss in the next chapter.

Naturally, other factors—nutrition, amount of sleep, childhood experiences, and all the many things that go to make up a person's life—also impact on the stress response. Attention to these areas will help you deal with stress.

Part of the following exercise for improving your coping skills involves using progressive muscle relaxation. Try it once or twice to become familiar with it before applying it.

For full benefits, set aside around thirty minutes a day for several days in a row to practice this exercise. The first step is to make a list of the things in your life that cause you to feel stressed—even minor things. You might have twenty or thirty things or situations on your list—for example, delivering a report to your boss, driving on the freeway, talking to your mother-in-law, worrying about your child's health.

Now go through the list and give each situation a "stress rating" from zero to one hundred—the more stress you feel, the higher the rating. Now rewrite the list to put it in order of stress, beginning with the lowest rating situations (i.e., the least difficult ones), and ending with the highest.

You are now ready to begin the rehearsal. Start with the first situation on your list (the least difficult one). Visualize yourself in that situation until the image is clear and detailed. See the room or place where the situation is occurring, and how it is furnished or arranged. Who else is there? Hear the sounds in that place, or what other people are saying. Run through your own actions in your mind. Hold the image of the situation for thirty or forty seconds. Do you feel the beginnings of any tension or anxiety in your body? If you do, that sensation is your signal to begin the progressive muscle relaxation. Take three deep, slow breaths and continue with the muscle tensing and relaxing. Continue to imagine the situation while you relax away the tension, using any sensation of tension as your signal to recommence the muscle relaxation technique.

The goal is to be able to visualize the situation for two periods of around twenty seconds each while keeping your body relaxed. When you are able to do this, you are ready to move on to the next situation on your list; repeat the process until your thirty minutes for that day's exercise is up. Over a period of several days, move through the whole list, including the most difficult situation.

This exercise will teach you a lot about the way your system reacts to stress, and where the tension manifests itself in your body. It will also help you rehearse how to respond in a relaxed way in real situations, and give you more confidence in facing them. You can use it in combination with the techniques of using realistic automatic thoughts described in the next chapter, for an added degree of effectiveness.

Finally, remember to reward yourself when you face difficult situations. Focus on the positive aspects of your achievements, and use encouraging self-talk—such as, "You did that part really well"—instead of criticizing yourself for the things you did wrong. Even if you feel you did nothing right in a given situation, remember that it took courage to face it in the first place. Getting into the habit of rewarding instead of criticizing yourself reduces your anxiety about future stressors.

Recommended Reading

The Relaxation and Stress Reduction Workbook, 3rd ed., by Martha Davis, Elizabeth Robins Echelon, and Matthew McKay (Oakland, Calif.: New Harbinger Publications, 1988), has excellent chapters on meditation and relaxation, not to mention self-hypnosis, coping skills training, assertiveness training, and more. I highly recommend this book.

✦

CHAPTER 18

THOUGHT

Our mind
And every kind of jewel:
If you polish them
They will shine
Accordingly.
—*JAPANESE FOLK ZEN SAYING*

Susan's Story

THINGS were just not working out the way Susan had hoped. She was by nature an optimistic, energetic person. For the last twenty-five years, though, she had been in a difficult marriage. Her husband had been unfaithful to her, and they argued constantly about everything. Now that the children had left home, things seemed to get worse since they no longer had a buffer between them.

Susan was very much into spiritual and New Age beliefs. She believed very strongly, for instance, that we create our own realities, and that we are 100 percent responsible for everything that happens to us.

So, when she had started to feel depressed, she had proceeded to immerse herself in the positive thinking methods promoted by various New Age gurus. She was convinced that she was 100 percent responsible for the state of her marriage, and that she could create a better reality for herself if only she could think the "right" thoughts.

Unfortunately, however, no amount of positive thinking on her part could change the fact that her husband behaved thoughtlessly toward her and that their relationship was difficult. Believing she was totally responsible only made her feel worse. Furthermore, she saw her inability to solve her problems through "right" thinking as yet another personal failure. Her health began to deteriorate. She came down with chronic sinusitis, and her asthma worsened—signs that her immune system was in chaos. Her depression also became worse and worse.

After I got to know her, I pointed out to her that many people have disagreed with those New Age ideas, since in many cases they amount to little more than blaming the victim. It would be callous and cruel, for example, to tell a starving child in Ethiopia that he had created his own reality of poverty and deprivation. "I needed to hear that," she told me. Starting at that time, she began to take realistic steps to improve her situation: She convinced her husband to get counseling, and both of them set off to learn improved communication skills, as they were determined to save their marriage.

In addition to couple counseling, Susan saw a psychologist for cognitive therapy to explore further her self-concept and beliefs. She discovered that she tended to see things in very black-and-white terms, and that this often led her to react to events in a rigid way, setting her up for depression. Susan had a basically resilient personality, so she made very quick progress in therapy and was able to quite easily make the transition to a more realistic way of dealing with her circumstances in life.

This, along with an intensive course of supportive therapies, including yoga, light therapy, and supplemental vitamins and minerals, led to a gradual improvement in her many physical complaints as well as her depression. When I last saw her she was feeling physically and emotionally well, full of energy, and along with her husband had made real progress in redefining and repairing their marriage.

Susan's story highlights an issue that is quite common: the desire to be in control. The New Age idea about us being 100 percent responsible for everything that happens to us really reflects our desire to have control over our lives. If we believe ourselves to be in control, we feel more secure, and more empowered to change our situation if necessary. Realistically, though, there are many factors in our lives that are beyond our complete control, like the behavior of others.

Psychologists once thought that the degree to which people feel in control of events in their lives was a measure of how healthy they were. The more control they felt they had, the healthier they were thought to be. Interestingly, recent studies of human immune functioning do not bear this out. Instead, they suggest the opposite: People with a strong belief in their ability to control events have worse immune functioning. In addition, if these people experience any difficulties in their lives, their immune functioning deteriorates greatly. What this suggests is that if a person believes herself to be in control of—and hence responsible for—all the problems around her, she becomes much more easily stressed and unwell than a person with a less self-centered view of the world.[1]

Studies have also shown that people who would rather control others than be friendly with them have poor immune functioning. On the other hand, people who show extremely high levels of restraint or self-inhibition around others also have decreased immunity.[2] In other words, when it comes to dealing with other people, the healthiest situation seems to be when you can express your needs, but not to the point of demanding control over others. That way, you respect both your own needs and theirs. And of course, that is the basis for true friendship. So we see: Friendship is healthy and healing.

What all of these studies, and Susan's story, show us is that your beliefs and ways of thinking have a real power to affect your body, your mood, and the way you interact with others. You can use this power to help you recover. In this chapter, we'll look at some specific ways to do this.

Harnessing the Strength of Thought

As Susan's story demonstrates, severe depression, affecting you from your emotions all the way down to the cellular level, can arise partly from the way you think. Of course, this is not to say that depression is "all in your head," or that the problems in your life aren't real. Researchers and therapists know from their years of experience, though, that people with depression often unintentionally add to their own troubles by thinking about things in unrealistic ways. And because they are not seeing things realistically, it becomes much more difficult for them to solve their problems.

Cognitive therapy is the name given to a specific type of psychotherapy that deals with thoughts and styles of thinking. Many studies have shown that cognitive therapy is highly effective; in fact, it has been proven to be superior to medication both for the treatment of depression and for the prevention of relapses.[3] Many doctors are unaware of this, and do not refer patients to psychotherapists when they should. As a treatment, it complements medication well, and I believe that most people on antidepressants should be using it.

In this chapter I'll present some of the key ideas behind cognitive therapy. Through simple but challenging exercises, you'll learn ways to identify and change the unrealistic negative beliefs that are holding you back from recovery.

Automatic Thoughts

Most of our thinking goes on without us being consciously in control of it. We are constantly talking to ourselves in our minds, and much of the time we are not fully aware of it. Our inner "self-talk" goes on automatically, without deliberate effort. These automatic thoughts provide a sort of background climate to our daily activities. They color our experiences and determine how we react emotionally to them.

Since we are often unaware of our automatic thoughts, we tend to believe that it is our experiences alone that are responsible for how we feel. In fact, it is the tone of our automatic thoughts that is really responsible for how we feel emotionally.

Consider this example: A woman delivered a lecture, did a very good job of it, and yet felt painfully anxious throughout it. She assumed that the lecture itself caused the anxiety, but she was ignoring the role played by the automatic thoughts that were going through her head at the time. Her automatic thoughts, operating at a low level of conscious awareness, were saying things like, "I haven't made this lecture interesting enough for the students. They'll get bored. They'll see that I'm nervous, and I'll be humiliated. I'll feel awful—I might have to run out of here and escape . . . I'm just a complete failure . . ." and so on. Even though these automatic thoughts were unrealistic—not representing the objective situation—they were very emotionally distressing. The lecture itself went well, but she felt anxious because of her automatic thoughts.

The key thing to understand is that *on an emotional level, we cannot tell the difference between realistic and unrealistic thoughts.* For example, no matter how successful we are, if we tell ourselves that we're failures, we will feel emotionally like failures.

The first two goals of cognitive therapy are to become aware of the things we tell ourselves automatically, and then to maintain a healthy skepticism about them. We need to determine if those thoughts are realistic or not. Some of them will be, but many will probably represent distortions of reality, as in the case of the lecturer. Distortions of reality are the cause of much needless misery.

We can instead choose to adopt more realistic automatic thoughts. This does not mean replacing all your negative thoughts with positive ones, like many of the power of positive thinking gurus would have you do. That would only be another way of distorting reality. To deal with situations in life most effectively, we need to see them as realistically as possible.

Becoming Conscious of Your Inner World

It takes conscious effort to become aware of automatic thoughts. It is a skill that takes practice to learn. When you're feeling anxious or depressed, you may be totally unaware of the automatic thoughts that are responsible for your mood. Bringing them into focus requires that you distance yourself temporarily from your emotions, and become an observer of the processes going on in your mind.

This is how you can do this: When you are in the midst of a moment of special anxiety or depression, stop what you're doing and ask yourself, "What am I saying to myself right now?" Try running through the details of the situation you were thinking about, and asking yourself what it is about it that concerns you. Keep a small notepad with you, and write down the troubling automatic thoughts. Use your feelings of anxiety or depression as your signal to go through this exercise then and there. Respect your feelings, and let them teach you about your automatic thoughts.

If you find you're so caught up in your feelings that you can't stop to do this exercise, you can instead do the progressive muscle relaxation exercise in the previous chapter, and then try again.

Common Types of Distortions

The next step is to evaluate the automatic thoughts you've uncovered. Therapists have found that the automatic thoughts of depressed people tend to contain particular types of distortions.[4]

You may find that your own automatic thoughts fall into one of these common patterns:

Overgeneralizing: For example, a person might miss his bus one day and say to himself, "I'm totally unorganized." This thought is unrealistic because it ignores the many things this person has managed to do in an organized manner, like catching the bus on other days, doing his shopping, dressing himself, and so on. "Always" statements are another form of overgeneralization. For example, the lecturer mentioned earlier might say, "I *always* make a mess of things," thus making a global statement about her whole life based on only one incident. That would be a serious distortion of reality, and a very painful one.

All-or-nothing thinking: This is similar to overgeneralizing. For example, a person might feel that unless everybody loves her, she is totally unlovable—all or nothing. Or she might feel that unless she does everything perfectly, she is a complete failure. This type of thinking is also very hurtful to oneself.

Looking only at the negative side: When a person is depressed, he tends to selectively pay attention to only the negative aspects of his situation. He might, for example, spend all his time thinking about his debts, and refuse to see all the good things in life he's achieved.

Jumping to conclusions: For example, the lecturer might see a student in the back of the room looking tired and jump to the conclusion that she is boring them. In doing so, she doesn't even consider the very real possibilities that the student was up late the night before studying or partying, or is getting over a cold, or whatever.

Taking responsibility for things that are unrealistically beyond one's direct control: For example, a person might think, "If only I'd been a better kid, Mom wouldn't have been an alcoholic," or "If only I hadn't let my friend drive that day, they wouldn't have been in that accident." This type of thinking is very unfair to yourself.

Being Your Own Philosopher

Evaluating your automatic thoughts is a bit like being a philosopher. You search for the truth, and examine things in a detached way, just as they do.

Take each automatic thought on its own, and ask yourself these four questions about it:[5]

1. *What evidence do I have that this thought is true?* For example, the lecturer could have asked this question about her thought, "I am a complete failure." If she had, she would have realized that there was almost no real evidence to support it, but much evidence to refute it.
2. *How else could I view this situation?* The lecturer could have said to herself, "Well, maybe the subject is boring to some students, but I'm giving it a good try to make it interesting. I'll bet at least some of them are interested."
3. *Realistically, what is the worst thing that could happen here, and what would it mean for my life?* This question helps you keep things in a proper perspective. Here the lecturer would have seen that, even if the worst-case scenario happened, and she felt humiliated and had to run out of the class, it probably would have had little or no effect on her life in the long term. People might have been concerned that she was feeling unwell, or perhaps might have suggested that she take a few days off.
4. *Even if my depressing thoughts are realistic, what can I do to improve the situation?* This question is about approaching

things in a constructive way, instead of indulging in harmful feelings of helplessness and passivity. For example, the teacher could pass out evaluation forms to obtain some feedback about how her lectures were really perceived.

Each time you feel a strong emotion, focus on your automatic thoughts, write them down, and ask these four questions about them. Write down your answers, too, providing realistic responses to the automatic thoughts.

Uncovering Your True Beliefs

After doing the above exercise a few times, you may start noticing a pattern emerging. You may find that your automatic thoughts have similar themes and similar implications. This similarity occurs because the various automatic thoughts come from the same source—from an underlying belief. If you look at the lecturer's thoughts, for instance, their underlying source was the belief: "I must do everything perfectly, and satisfy everybody, or I have totally failed."

Her therapist pointed out this implication to her. When she heard it, she was surprised, because she knew in her heart that she didn't really think that way—it was far too extreme a belief. "Well, maybe I really believe that I must do *most* things perfectly, and satisfy *most* people, in order to succeed," she said. Her true belief was much less harsh, and did not set her up for failure like the other one did.

If you are able to identify the beliefs implied by your automatic thoughts, you will sometimes find that you don't really believe what they are saying. Unrealistic automatic thoughts are often based on exaggerations or distortions of your true beliefs.

Sometimes, however, your automatic thoughts really are true reflections of your underlying beliefs. In that case, the underlying beliefs themselves, not just distortions of them, would be the source of your distress.

As an example, suppose the lecturer had said, "Yes, I really do believe that I must do everything perfectly, and satisfy everybody, or I have totally failed." In that case, she could become a philosopher again, and examine that belief in the light of reason. One way to objectively examine beliefs is to draw up a table comparing their advantages and disadvantages. Put a rating of importance, from zero (not important at all) to ten (extremely important), next to each advantage and disadvantage, and then tally up all the ratings. Here's how it might look:[6]

Belief: *I must do everything perfectly, and satisfy everybody, or I have totally failed.*

Advantages of This Belief	Disadvantages of This Belief
1. It makes me work my hardest and behave nicely to everybody. (Importance = 10)	1. It makes me very vulnerable to the slightest mistakes, and to people's likes and dislikes. (Importance = 10)
2. People will think I'm good at what I do, and nice, too. (Importance = 10)	2. Since everybody wants different things, I end up having to be different things to different people. (Importance = 8)
3. I'll have many friends and admirers. (10)	3. To constantly satisfy others, I often have to put their needs ahead of mine. (8)
	4. I need constant reassurance, since I can't always be certain everyone's satisfied. (9)
	5. I can't say what I really think, since that might

		not be what they want to hear. (9)	
		6. If someone is having a bad day and is in a bad mood, I think it's my fault, or at least that it's my job to fix it so that everyone is satisfied. (10)	
		7. It's impossible to do everything perfectly and satisfy everybody, so I can never really succeed. This makes me feel depressed. (10)	
Total: Advantages	30	Disadvantages	64

As you can see, this exercise can help you determine if the benefits of your belief are outweighed by its cost, as it was in the lecturer's case. If they are, it would be to your advantage to mellow the belief out. For example, the lecturer's belief could become "I'll do my best, but no human being is perfect."

Another way to evaluate your beliefs is to apply them to other people you know. For example, the lecturer could ask herself, "Can I think of people I know who are successful? Do *they* do absolutely everything perfectly? Have *they* ever made a mistake in their lives? Is it possible that someone was once dissatisfied with them? Do they ever say no to people?" And so on.

If you ask yourself these questions, you may find that you have two sets of standards: one for yourself, which is harsh and unforgiving, and one for others, which is far gentler and more realistic. This is common in people with depression. Treating yourself as you treat others means that you recognize that you, too, are a human being. You are allowed to have imperfections and make mistakes—we all do. And it's impossible to please everyone all the time. So be gentle on yourself.

Are Your Beliefs Your Own?

Another way of looking at beliefs is to ask, "Where did this belief come from?" or "Whose voice do I hear stating this belief?" Is it your own voice, or does it sound like a parent, or an obnoxious TV commercial? Many of our unhelpful beliefs are actually chosen unconsciously, accumulated from our family or culture, like junk mail piling up in the mailbox. For example, how about these common statements: Life isn't a bed of roses. Life's a bitch, then you die. If you're happy, something bad will happen. Life wasn't meant to be easy.

Ouch! Beliefs like those can be very limiting. Remember, you have the option of discarding or rewriting them. Ask yourself which beliefs you really claim as your own, and which are just baggage that you're unconsciously carrying around. Challenge these beliefs—you might surprise yourself.

Some people find it helpful to use books and tapes on affirmations to assist in the incorporation of more realistic beliefs. Reminding yourself of your true beliefs can be particularly useful as a coping technique if an old pattern of distress recurs. For example, during her next lecture, the lecturer could remind herself of some of the beliefs that she'd discovered were more true to herself than the old ones. (Further techniques for coping with stressful situations were discussed in the previous chapter.)

This chapter has presented just a few of the methods used by psychotherapists to treat depression. While self-help techniques are effective for some, they are much enhanced when undertaken with the assistance of a skilled counselor. Cognitive therapy, as I mentioned before, is proven to be more effective than medication. If you are depressed, or on long-term antidepressants to prevent a relapse, it makes sense for you to seek out a good psychotherapist.

Being with Others

The world is
Like a mirror, you see?
Smile, and your friends
Smile back.
—*JAPANESE FOLK ZEN SAYING*

All real living is meeting.—*MARTIN BUBER*

One of the most prominent features of depression is the tendency to want to withdraw from the world and isolate yourself. Even if you are not consciously aware of this tendency, it is reinforced by feelings of irritability and a low frustration threshold that make it difficult to be with others. This is a natural feature of the normal depressed response, as I discussed in the first chapter. It aids in focusing inward, which is an essential step in the internal transformation that is the goal of the depressed response.

If the depressed response fails and becomes chronic, as in a major depressive disorder, this tendency to withdraw and isolate yourself ends up becoming counterproductive. In major depressive disorder, being around other people is actually therapeutic. It helps you avoid dwelling unproductively on problems, and reinforces connections with external realities, helping to moderate the extremes of your moods.

Despite this, it can take great effort to be with others when you're depressed. It can at times seem too difficult to be worthwhile. If you find that this is the case, consider your social interactions as a powerful type of therapy, which, in reality, they are. All therapies require effort to be successful. If you understand that being with others is beneficial to your well-being, you will be more willing to make the effort.

You should definitely make sure that no more than two or three days at a time go by without some sort of close contact with other people, even if it's just a heart-to-heart talk on the phone with a friend or therapist.

Try to be patient and respectful to others. This might not be easy when you're feeling awful yourself, but if you're rude to others, they will have a harder time dealing with you, and may be rude back—and this can make you feel worse. So work on being kind to others—if not for their sake then for your own.

Be careful of using shopping as your way to interact with people when you're depressed. And it's a good idea to avoid making financial decisions when you're feeling down. You're more likely to overspend or to be pushed around by salespeople or agents.

Sometimes difficult interpersonal situations can be the cause of depression. In these cases, talking it out with the people involved, or a confidant, or a therapist is a good idea. By making the effort to be patient and respectful to other people, and learning how to moderate your own stress responses to interpersonal difficulties, you will acquire the healing advantages of social connectedness. This work is not only therapeutic in depression, it helps to prevent future relapses and renders you more resistant to illness in general.

Make a Schedule

When you're depressed, it's also a good idea for you to make a schedule of activities, or a list of things that need doing. Keeping active and accomplishing things, even minor things like answering mail or putting out the trash, is one of the best ways to alleviate sorrow. A schedule is an excellent tool to help you overcome the inertia and lack of motivation that are characteristic of major depressive disorder. Remember to schedule some fun things, too!

Recommended Reading

Self-Esteem: A Proven Program of Cognitive Techniques for Assessing, Improving, and Maintaining Your Self-Esteem, by Matthew McKay and Patrick Fanning (Oakland, Calif.: New Harbinger Publications, 1987), guides you step by step through learning how to talk back to self-critical automatic thoughts, see yourself more realistically, and have compassion on yourself. It is easy to read, use, and contains a good selection of self-help techniques.

Depression: The Way Out of Your Prison, by Dorothy Rowe (New York and London: Routledge, 1991), impressed me because of its down-to-earth wisdom. It is a discussion about some of the beliefs that, though held with the best of intentions, can end up trapping people in a state of depression.

YOUR STORY

The recurrent moments of crisis and decision when
understood, are growth junctures, points of initiation
which mark a release from one state of being
and a growth into the next.
—JILL PURCE

Where there is a way or path, it is someone else's.
Each of us has to find his own way.
—JOSEPH CAMPBELL

HEALING is part of your nature. It has been my aim in this book to help you understand how your depressed response can be a profoundly productive and transformative experience for you.

Sometimes it is hard to trust in the wisdom of your natural responses, especially when they are themselves painful and disorienting. But when you are depressed, your being is filled with potentiality as at no other time. Breaking down makes you capable of a truly deep-seated renewal, and of gaining an increased degree of self-understanding. You can come to a new inner synthesis that will enable you to deal with changed life circumstances, and even flourish. I have witnessed this happen with many people.

Even if your depressed response has gone on to become major depressive disorder, a complete healing is always possible. Your innate health-restoring mechanisms are only waiting to be nourished, like a tree waiting for rain.

You can nurture yourself with a mostly vegetarian whole-food diet, a good multivitamin and mineral supplement, and St. John's wort or amino acid therapy. Stay in touch with your body with regular gentle exercise, relaxation techniques, and some time spent outdoors in natural light.

You can enhance the creative problem-solving ability of your mind and spirit through dream analysis, meditation, play, keeping a journal, working with your automatic thoughts and underlying beliefs, and consciously applying the principles of the creative process. In addition to setting time aside for yourself, make a point of spending time with other people, and seek out a therapist to help you on your way. There are many effective, life-enhancing natural options for you to incorporate in your own holistic plan.

The essence of healing is the flow of creative energy that arises from the deepest levels of your life force. The therapies in this book will provide you with a solid grounding for this to occur. I encourage you to explore them, experiment with them, and discover what works best for you. You are a unique person, and your story is unlike any other.

Appendix 1

✦

Finding Practitioners of Natural Medicine

HOLISTIC MEDICINE

To locate a medical doctor in your area who practices according to the principles of natural or holistic medicine, call or write to:

American Holistic Medical Association
6728 Old McLean Village Drive
McLean, Virginia 22101-3906
Patient Information: 1-703-556-9728

For $5, you will be sent a listing of holistic physicians across the United States. This takes four to six weeks.

NATUROPATHIC MEDICINE

Naturopaths, or N.D.'s, offer an alternative to conventional medicine. They've kept alive a lot of natural healing techniques that otherwise might have been left by the wayside. Naturopaths employ a variety of treatments, including nutritional therapy, herbalism, homeopathy, acupuncture, and physical manipulation. They are not allowed to prescribe conventional drugs, but most of them would prefer not to anyway.

Naturopaths are now regulated in many states. In the past, the standard of naturopathic education was poor, but it has been making strides and gaining wide respect.

Naturopathic medicine is particularly good for treating chronic illnesses, where conventional medicine has failed. Naturopaths, however, are usually less adept at diagnosis than conventional doctors. You're better off seeing a conventional doctor, or a holistic doctor, to get a firm diagnosis before you consult a naturopath. Unfortunately, only one or two insurance companies will pay for their services.

To locate a good naturopathic physician in your area, contact:

American Association of Naturopathic Physicians
2366 Eastlake Avenue East, Suite 322
Seattle, WA 98102
Phone: 1-206-827-6035
Fax: 1-206-323-7612

For $5, they will mail you some brochures on naturopathic medicine, along with a list of licensed naturopaths across the United States.

Appendix 2

✦

Suppliers of St. John's Wort Extract

LIQUID EXTRACTS

Here's a list of some of the suppliers of St. John's wort extract, and where you can contact them. It's divided into sections for the United States, Canada, the United Kingdom, Europe, and Australia. This list is in no way comprehensive. I don't recommend one over any of the others. However, if you are allergic to corn or grains, you might do best to use the Eclectic Institute's hypoallergenic extract. If you're a strict vegetarian, you might want to use Nature's Answer, since they use vegetable glycerin (not animal glycerin) in the extraction process. Their product is also certified to be kosher.

UNITED STATES

    Eclectic Institute
    14385 SE Lusted Road
    Sandy, OR 97055-9549
    Phone: 1-800-332-4372
    Fax: 1-503-668-3227
    Organic, hypoallergenic—without corn or grain alcohol. Available in plain or black cherry flavor, with vitamin C.

    Gaia Herbs
    12 Landcaster County Road
    Harvard, MA 01451
    Phone: 1-800-831-7780
    Fax: 1-800-717-1722
    Extracted from flowers and buds only.

Herb Pharm
P.O. Box 116
Williams, OR 97544
Phone: 1-800-348-4372
Fax: 1-800-545-7392
Extracted from flowers and buds only.

McZand Herbal
P.O. Box 5312
Santa Monica, CA 90409
Phone: 1-800-800-0405
Fax: 1-310-822-1050
This extract is a little more expensive than most, but it appears to be more concentrated.

Nature's Answer
Hauppage, NY 11788
Ask your health-food store owner to order it for you—no sales directly to the public. Alcohol-free extract, with vegetable glycerin.

Nature's Plus
548 Broodhollow Road
Melville, NY 11747
Ask your health-food store owner to order it for you. This extract is standardized and made with vegetable glycerin.

Planetary Formulations
P.O. Box 533
Soquel, CA 95073
Phone: 1-800-776-7701
Fax: 1-408-438-7410
A more concentrated extract than most. Manufacturer recommends taking it three days on, two days off.

CANADA

Canadians can order from U.S. suppliers. Alternatively, here's a Canadian supplier who will ship anywhere:

Health Service Center
971 Bloor Street West
Toronto, Ontario 46H1L7
Phone or fax: 1-416-535-9562

UNITED KINGDOM

Baldwin's
173 Walworth Road
London SE 17 1RW
Phone: 44-0171-703-5550

EUROPE

In German-speaking countries, St. John's wort extract is available both
by prescription and as an over-the-counter medication. Ask for it at
your local doctor, pharmacy, or health-food store. Some of the trade
names are Esbericum, Hyperforat, Jarsin, Neurapas, Neuroplant,
Psychotonin M, and Sedariston. Here is a manufacturer of capsules
containing extract:

Lichwter Pharma GmbH.
Berlin, Germany
Phone: 49-30-403-700

AUSTRALIA

Many Australian suppliers will not sell directly to the public. You may
have to ask your health-food store owner or doctor/naturopath to
order it for you. Here are two companies who will sell extract directly
to you:

Herbal Supplies Pty. Ltd.
1–5 Jennifer Avenue
Ridgehaven, South Australia
Phone: 61-08-8263-2033 or 61-08-8265-4777
Fax: 61-08-8263-2033

MediHerb
124 McEvoy Street
Warwick, Queensland 4370
Phone: 61-07-661-0700
Fax: 61-07-661-5656

SUPPLIERS OF CAPSULES (UNITED STATES)

Depending on the brand, taking capsules of St. John's wort may be considerably less expensive than the extract. However, in my opinion, capsules are not the best form to take. See Chapter 11 for further details.

Nutrition Headquarters, Inc.
One Nutrition Plaza
Carbondale, IL 62901-8825
Fax: 1-618-529-4553
Postal or fax orders only. Guaranteed potency herb, capsules standardized for hypericin content.

Eclectic Institute.
Freeze-dried herbal extracts. See under "Extract" for address and phone number. These capsules are not standardized.

Hypericum Buyer's Club
8205 Santa Monica Boulevard, Suite 472
Los Angeles, CA 90046
Phone: 1-888-497-3742
The distributors state that these capsules are the same type as was used in many of the studies on depression.

APPENDIX 3

✦

Where to Find Bright-Light Units

Light visors, tabletop light units, and dawn simulators are available through:

Bio-Brite, Inc.
7315 Wisconsin Avenue, Suite 1300W
Bethesda, MD 20814-3202
Phone: 1-800-621-5483 or 1-301-961-8557
Fax: 1-301-961-6407

Light visors, tabletop and freestanding light units, and dawn simulators are available through:

The Sun Box Co.
19217 Orbit Drive
Gaithersburg, MD 20879-4149
Phone: 1-800-548-3968 or 1-301-869-5980
Fax: 1-301-977-2281

Tube-shaped skylight kits made by several companies and costing less than $200 are available in many hardware stores. The manufacturers state that you can install them yourself in about two hours.

APPENDIX 4

✦

A Low-Stress Antiallergy Diet

Many people are intolerant of common foods because of allergies, hereditary enzyme deficiency, hormonal individuality, or for other reasons. This intolerance can cause a variety of physical and emotional symptoms. Because the offending food items may be those that are eaten every day, many people do not make the connection between their symptoms and the particular food. The purpose of an elimination diet is to stop eating foods to which you may be sensitive and then to reintroduce them one by one to determine their effects on you.

During the period of food avoidance, standard elimination diets usually restrict people to just a few foods that are said to be well tolerated by almost everyone, like white rice, lamb, and a few vegetables. In practice, such a severely restricted diet can make life miserable, and so I don't recommend you undertake it if you are currently depressed. Instead, I have provided simplified recommendations designed to remove the two most common food offenders: gluten and dairy products.

Health-food stores and many groceries carry products for people with food allergies or sensitivities, like gluten-free pasta or cereal and soy milk. You should not have much trouble finding these replacement foods.

Before you begin your diet, write down those symptoms that you want to modify. Try following this diet for ten days or so, and see if there are any improvements. Commonly, symptoms are aggravated in the first few days, as your system craves the foods on which it has become dependent. If you notice no improvement over a week, you are probably not sensitive to milk or gluten.

If you do notice improvements, reintroduce milk first, to test your response. If your response is excessive, you may be able to alleviate it by swallowing a weak solution of baking soda, or some Alka Seltzer Gold. (Obviously, if the reaction is severe, you should see your doctor straightaway.) Wait another two days to determine if you have a

delayed response to the milk. If you have no response, try reintroduc-
ing wheat.

Other common food intolerances are to corn, eggs, and citrus fruits,
so you might want to try eliminating those for a week. If you discover
you are sensitive to a food, avoid it. You may be able to reintroduce it
cautiously in a year's time or so. Avoiding a food for a long period of
time often decreases your sensitivity to it.

Avoid (for Ten Days)	Use Instead
All dairy products, including:	
Milk	Soy, rice, or nut milk
Butter/dairy spreads	Tahini, hummus, blended tofu spreads, almond or cashew paste, etc.; canola, flax, or olive oil
Gluten, found in:	
Wheat, rye, barley, oats, spelt	Rice, buckwheat, millet, soy, arrowroot, or potato flour, tapioca, amaranth, quinoa

APPENDIX 5

✦

Azo Food Dyes

Azo food dyes are the coloring agents used in many soft drinks, cordials, hard candies, and other foods. They disrupt the production of neurotransmitters, thus possibly contributing to depression (see Chapter 13).

Additive Code	Name
102	Tartrazine*
107	Yellow 2G
110	Sunset yellow FCF*
122	Azorubine, carmoisine
123	Amaranth*
124	Ponceau 4R, Brilliant scarlet*
151	Brilliant black BN, Black PN
155	Brown HT*

Those marked with an asterisk (*) are the more commonly used ones.

Appendix 6

✦

Foods to Avoid When Taking MAOIs

Monoamine oxidase inhibitors, or MAOIs, are a type of antidepressant medication and are described in Chapter 10. MAOIs interact with an amino acid called tyramine, contained in many different foods, causing high blood pressure.

As I discussed in Chapter 11, one of the ways that the herb St. John's wort works is through a MAOI-like effect. This effect is very weak, so it isn't necessary to restrict your diet while taking the herb. However, if you already have high blood pressure, and your doctor okays your use of St. John's wort, I recommend you follow these dietary restrictions for an extra margin of safety.

Do not use: alcohol; fava or broad beans; cheese (except cream cheese or cottage cheese); liver; pickled or smoked fish, meat, or poultry; sausage; packaged soups; orange pulp; yeast or meat extracts (including Bovril, Marmite, or yeast vitamin supplements).

Have no more than one or two servings a day of: soy sauce, sour cream, yogurt, bananas, plums, raisins, tomatoes, eggplant, avocados.

You should also be certain not to mix MAOIs or St. John's wort with any of the medications mentioned in Chapter 11. Consult the information provided by your doctor and/or with your MAOI medication for further details.

APPENDIX 7

For the Health Professional:
Review Articles on St. John's Wort

There have been dozens of published clinical studies on the use of St. John's wort in depression. The following articles each provide a review, critique, and summary of them.

Ernst, E. "St. John's Wort, an Antidepressant—A Systematic, Criteria-Based Review." *Phytomedicine* 2, no. 1 (July 1995): 67–71.

Harrer, G., and V. Schulz. "Clinical Investigation of the Antide-pressant Effectiveness of Hypericum." *Journal of Geriatric Psychiatry and Neurology* 7 Suppl. 1 (October 1994): S 6–8.

Linde, K., et al. "St. John's Wort for Depression—An Overview and Meta-Analysis of Randomised Clinical Trials." *British Medical Journal* 313, no. 7052 (August 3, 1996): 253–58.

NOTES

✦

INTRODUCTION

1. This term was coined by Swedish psychoanalyst Dr. Emmy Gut in her book *Productive and Unproductive Depression: Success or Failure of a Vital Process* (London: Tavistock/Routledge, 1989).

CHAPTER 1. HEALING TRANSFORMATIONS

1. N. M. Graham et al., "Adverse Effects of Aspirin, Acetaminophen, and Ibuprofen on Immune Function, Viral Shedding, and Clinical Status in Rhinovirus-Infected Volunteers," *Journal of Infectious Diseases* 162, no. 6 (1990): 1277–82.

2. G. Harrer and V. Schulz, "Clinical Investigation of the Antidepressant Effectiveness of Hypericum," *Journal of Geriatric Psychiatry and Neurology* 7 Suppl. 1 (October 1994): S 6–8; D. Johnson et al., "Effects of Hypericum Extract LI 160 Compared with Maprotiline on Resting EEG and Evoked Potentials in 24 Volunteers," *Journal of Geriatric Psychiatry and Neurology* 7 Suppl. 1 (October 1994): S 44–46.

3. Johnson et al., "Effects of Hypericum Extract LI 160."

CHAPTER 2. DREAMS

1. F. B. Linderman, *Pretty Shield: Medicine Woman of the Crow* (Lincoln: University of Nebraska Press, 1932), p. 166; quoted in: L. Irwin, *The Dream Seekers: Native American Visionary Traditions of the Great Plains* (Norman: University of Oklahoma Press, 1994).

2. R. F. Fortune, *Omaha Secret Societies* (New York: Columbia University Press, 1932), p. 42; quoted in: Irwin, see 1.

3. L. Irwin, *The Dream Seekers: Native American Visionary Traditions of the Great Plains* (Norman: University of Oklahoma Press, 1994).

4. H. Fiss, "Experimental Strategies for the Study of the Function of Dreaming," in *The Mind in Sleep: Psychology and Psychophysiology*, 2nd ed., edited by S. J. Ellman and J. S. Antrobus (New York: John Wiley and Sons, 1991).

5. Ibid.

6. Irwin, *Dream Seekers*, p. 83.

7. J. Winson, *Brain and Psyche: The Biology of the Unconscious* (Garden City, N.Y.: Doubleday, 1985).

8. *Talmud Sanhedrin* 30a, *Berachos* 55a and b, etc.

9. Rabbi Chaim ibn Attar (1696–1743), *Or HaChaim Bereishis* 28:12, 37:7, and 41:1, discussed in M. Zlotowitz, *Bereishis*, vol. 1b (New York: Mesorah Publications, 1977), pp. 1593–99.

10. J. Fire and R. Erdoes, *Lame Deer: Seeker of Visions* (New York: Simon and Schuster, 1972), p. 65, quoted in Irwin, *Dream Seekers*.

11. Irwin, *Dream Seekers*.

12. L. N. Weinstein, D. G. Schwartz, and A. M. Arkin, "Qualitative Aspects of Sleep Mentation" in Ellman and Antrobus, *The Mind in Sleep*, pp. 172–212.

13. S. J. Ellman et al., "REM Deprivation: A Review" in Ellman and Antrobus, *The Mind in Sleep*, pp. 329–76.

14. H. Schulz and M. Jobert, "Effects of Hypericum Extract on the Sleep EEG in Older Volunteers," *Journal of Geriatric Psychiatry and Neurology* 7 Suppl 1 (October 1994): S 39–43.

15. Hiss, "Experimental Strategies."

CHAPTER 3. THE SOUL'S VISION

1. D. Baker and E. Nestor, *Depression* (Basingstoke, Eng.: Marshalls, 1984).

2. M. Buber, "God and the World's Evil" in *Contemporary Jewish Thought: A Reader*, edited by S. Noveck (New York: B'nai B'rith, 1963), p. 257.

3. A. L. Kroeber, "The Arapaho," *Anthropological Papers of the American Museum of Natural History* 18 (1904): 433, quoted in *The Dream Seekers: Native American Visionary Traditions of the Great Plains*, edited by L. Irwin (Norman: University of Oklahoma Press, 1994), p. 76.

4. D. J. Benor, "Survey of Spiritual Healing Research," *Complementary Medical Research* 4, no. 3 (September 1990): 9–33.

5. W. P. Smith, W. C. Compton, and W. B. West, "Meditation as an Adjunct to a Happiness Enhancement Program," *Journal of Clinical Psychology* 51, no. 2 (March 1995): 269–73. D. L. Beauchamp-Turner and D. M. Levinson, "Effects of Meditations on Stress, Health, and Affect," *Medical Psychotherapy: An International Journal* 5 (1992): 123–31. J. Kabat-Zinn et al., "Effectiveness of a Meditation-Based Stress Reduction Program in the Treatment of Anxiety Disorders," *American Journal of Psychiatry* 149, no. 7 (July 1992): 936–43.

6. J. D. Teasdale, Z. Segal, and J. M. G. Williams, "How Does Cognitive Therapy Prevent Relapse and Why Should Attentional Control (Mindfulness) Training Help?" *Behavior Research and Therapy;* 33 no. 1 (1995): 25–39.

7. J. Gartner, D. Larson, and G. Allen, "Religious Commitment and Mental Health: A Review of the Empirical Literature," *Journal of Psychology and Theology* 19, no. 1 (1991): 6–25.

8. See e.g., Sigmund Freud, *The Future of an Illusion* (1927).

9. D. Lukoff, F. Lu, and R. Turner, "Toward a More Culturally Sensitive DSM-IV: Psychoreligious and Psychospiritual Problems," *Journal of Nervous and Mental Diseases* 180 (1992): 673–82.

10. Gartner et al., "Religious Commitment and Mental Health."

11. Ibid.

CHAPTER 4. ENTERING THE HEART OF CREATIVITY

1. B. L. Green, C. Wehling, and G. J. Talsky, "Group Art Therapy as an Adjunct to Treatment for Chronic Outpatients," *Hospital and Community Psychiatry* 38, no. 9 (September 1987): 988–91.

2. S. B. Hanser, and L. W. Thompson, "Effects of a Music Therapy Strategy on Older Adults," *Journal of Gerontology* 49, no. 6 (November 1994): 265–69. V. N. Stratton and A. H. Zalanowski, "Affective Impact of Music vs. Lyrics," *Empirical Studies of the Arts* 12, no. 2 (1994): 173–84. V. N. Stratton and A. H. Zalanowski, "The Effects of Music on Cognition and Mood," *Psychology of Music* 19, no. 2 (1991): 121–27. U. Reinhardt and E. Lange, "Effects of Music on Depressed Persons," *Psychiatrie, Neurologie and Medizinische Psychologie* 34, no. 7 (July 1982): 414–21.

3. Reinhardt and Lange, "Effects of Music on Depressed Persons."

4. Stratton and Zalanowski, "Affective Impact of Music vs. Lyrics."

5. J. Friedlander, "The Write Stuff," *New Woman* (Australia), November 1995, pp. 62–65.

CHAPTER 5. CREATIVE SOLUTIONS

1. Frederic Flach, *Resilience—Discovering a New Strength at Times of Stress* (New York: Fawcett Columbine, 1988).

CHAPTER 6. THE UNRESOLVED RESPONSE

1. Table adapted from *DSM-IV, Diagnostic and Statistical Manual of the American Psychiatric Association* (Washington, D.C.: American Psychiatric Association, 1993).

2. H. I. Kaplan, B. J. Sadock, and J. A. Grebb, *Kaplan and Sadock's Synopsis of Psychiatry*, 7th ed. (Baltimore: Williams and Wilkins, 1994).

3. Ibid.

CHAPTER 7. MIND AND BODY

1. T. B. Herbert and S. Cohen, "Depression and Immunity: A Meta-Analytic Review," *Psychological Bulletin* 113, no. 3 (1993): 472–86.

2. Ibid. M. Maes et al., "Relationships Between Interleukin-6 Activity, Acute Phase Proteins, and the Function of the Hypothalamic-Pituitary-Adrenal Axis in Severe Depression," *Psychiatry Research* 49, no. 1 (October 1993): 11–27. N. Muller et al., "Investigations of the Cellular Immunity During Depression and the Free Interval: Evidence for an Immune Activation in Affective Psychosis," *Progress in Neuropsychopharmacology and Biological Psychiatry* 17, no. 5 (September 1993): 713–30. D. Marazziti et al., "Immune Cell Imbalance in Major Depressive and Panic Disorders," *Neuropsychobiology* 26, no. 1–2 (1992): 23–26. M. Maes et al., "Immune Disorders in Depression: Higher T Helper / T Suppressor-Cytotoxic Cell Ratio," *Acta Psychiatrica Scandinavia* 86, no. 6 (December 1992): 423–31. C. S. Weisse, "Depression and Immunocompetence: A Review of the Literature," *Psychological Bulletin* 111, no. 3 (May 1992): 475–89. M. Maes et al., "Evidence for a Systemic Immune Activation During Depression: Results of Leukocyte Enumeration by Flow Cytometry in

Conjunction with Monoclonal Antibody Staining," *Psychological Medicine* 22 (1992): 45–53.

CHAPTER 8. MEDICAL MYSTERY TOUR

1. F. N. Pitts, R. E. Allen, and A. D. Allen, "Antibodies to the Early Antigen of the Epstein-Barr Virus in Relation to Major Depression" in *Depressive Disorders and Immunity*, edited by A. H. Miller (Washington, D.C.: American Psychiatric Press, 1989), pp. 171–89.

2. C. O. Truss, "The Role of Candida Albicans in Human Illness," *Journal of Orthomolecular Psychiatry* 10, no. 4 (1981): 228–38.

3. J. J. Murphy, S. Heptinstall, and J. R. A. Mitchell, "Randomized Double-Blind Placebo-Controlled Trial of Feverfew in Migraine Prevention," *Lancet*, July 23, 1988, pp. 189–92.

4. S. M. Hall et al., "Nicotine, Negative Affect, and Depression," *Journal of Consulting and Clinical Psychology* 61, no. 5 (October 1993): 761–67. J. C. Newman and F. J. Holden, "The 'Cerebral Diabetes' Paradigm for Unipolar Depression," *Medical Hypotheses* 41, no. 5 (1993): 391–408.

5. L. Christensen and R. Burrows, "Dietary Treatment of Depression," *Behavioural Therapy* 21 (1990): 183–93. K. Krietsch, L. Christensen, and B. White, "Prevalence, Presenting Symptoms, and Psychological Characteristics of Individuals Experiencing a Diet-Related Mood Disturbance," *Behavioural Therapy* 19 (1988): 593–604. R. Cacciatore et al. "Episodic Headache, Diminished Performance and Depressive Mood," *Schweizerische Rundschau Medizin Praxis* 85, no. 22 (May 28, 1996): 727–29.

CHAPTER 9. ON FINDING A THERAPIST

1. L. Davis, *The Courage to Heal Workbook* (New York: Harper and Row, 1990), p. 44.

2. Ibid., p. 48.

CHAPTER 10. THE PLACE FOR MEDICATION

1. Peter Kramer, *Listening to Prozac* (New York: Viking, 1993).

2. H. I. Kaplan, B. J. Sadock, and J. A. Grebb, *Kaplan and Sadock's Synopsis of Psychiatry*, 7th ed. (Baltimore: Williams and Wilkins, 1994), p. 978.

3. P. A. Childs et al., "Effect of Fluoxetine on Melatonin in Patients with Seasonal Affective Disorder and Matched Controls," *British Journal of Psychiatry* 166, no. 2 (February 1995): 196–98.
4. Kaplan et al., *Kaplan and Sadock's Synopsis of Psychiatry*.
5. Ibid., pp. 993–98.
6. Ibid., p. 1003.

CHAPTER 11. HERBAL MEDICINE

1. G. Lavie et al., "The Chemical and Biological Properties of Hypericin—Compound with a Broad Spectrum of Biological Activities," *Medicinal Research Reviews* 15, no. 2 (March 1995): 111–19. J. B. Hudson, I. Lopez-Bazzocchi, and G. H. Towers, "Antiviral Activities of Hypericin," *Antiviral Research* 15, no. 2 (February 1991): 101–12. M. Castleman, *The Healing Herbs* (Melbourne: Schwartz Books, 1991), pp. 321–25.
2. G. Harrer and V. Schulz, "Clinical Investigation of the Antidepressant Effectiveness of Hypericum," *Journal of Geriatric Psychiatry and Neurology* 7 Suppl. 1 (October 1994): S 6–8. H. Sommer and G. Harrer, "Placebo-Controlled Double-Blind Study Examining the Effectiveness of an Hypericum Preparation in 105 Mildly Depressed Patients," *Journal of Geriatric Psychiatry and Neurology* 7 Suppl. 1 (October 1994): S 9–11. W. D. Hubner, S. Lande, and H. Podzuweit, "Hypericum Treatment of Mild Depressions with Somatic Symptoms," *Journal of Geriatric Psychiatry and Neurology* 7 Suppl. 1 (October 1994): S 12–14. K. D. Hansgen, J. Vesper, and M. Ploch, "Multicenter Double-Blind Study Examining the Antidepressant Effectiveness of the Hypericum Extract LI 160," *Journal of Geriatric Psychiatry and Neurology* 7 Suppl. 1 (October 1994): S 15–18. E. U. Vorbach, W. D. Hubner, and K. H. Arnoldt, "Effectiveness and Tolerance of the Hypericum Extract LI 160 in Comparison with Imipramine: Randomized Double-Blind Study with 135 Outpatients," *Journal of Geriatric Psychiatry and Neurology* 7 Suppl. 1 (October 1994): S 19–23. G. Harrer, W. D. Hubner, and H. Podzuweit, "Effectiveness and Tolerance of the Hypericum Extract LI 160 Compared to Maprotiline: A Multicenter Double-Blind Study," *Journal of Geriatric Psychiatry and Neurology* 7 Suppl. 1 (October 1994): S 24–28. B. Martinez, S. Kasper, S. Ruhrmann, and H. J. Moller, "Hypericum in

the Treatment of Seasonal Affective Disorders," *Journal of Geriatric Psychiatry and Neurology* 7 Suppl. 1 (October 1994): S 29–33. H. Woelk, G. Burkard, and J. Grunwald, "Benefits and Risks of the Hypericum Extract LI 160: Drug Monitoring Study with 3250 Patients," *Journal of Geriatric Psychiatry and Neurology* 7 Suppl. 1 (October 1994): S 34–38.

3. K. Linde et al., "St John's Wort for Depression—An Overview and Meta-Analysis of Randomised Clinical Trials," *British Medical Journal* 313 (1996): 253–58.

4. Vorbach et al., "Effectiveness and Tolerance."

5. Harrer and Schulz, "Clinical Investigation."

6. D. Johnson et al., "Effects of Hypericum Extract LI 160 Compared with Maprotiline on Resting EEG and Evoked Potentials in 24 Volunteers," *Journal of Geriatric Psychiatry and Neurology* 7 Suppl. 1 (October 1994): S 44–46.

7. Woelk et al., "Benefits and Risks of the Hypericum Extract LI 160."

8. H. Bloomfield, M. Nordfors, and P. McWilliams, *Hypericum and Depression* (Santa Monica, Calif.: Prelude Press, 1996).

9. W. E. G. Muller and R. Rossol, "Effects of Hypericum Extract on the Expression of Serotonin Receptors," *Journal of Geriatric Psychiatry and Neurology* 7 Suppl. 1 (October 1994): S 63–64. S. Perovic and W. E. G. Muller, "Pharmacological Profile of Hypericum Extract: Effect on Scrotonin Uptake by Postsynaptic Receptors," *Arzneimittel Forschung* 45, no. 11 (November 1995): 1145 48.

10. O. Suzuki et al., "Inhibition of Monoamine Oxidase by Hypericin," *Planta Medica* 50, no. 3 (June 1984): 272–74.

11. H. M. Thiele and A. Walper, "Inhibition of MAO and COMT by Hypericum Extracts and Hypericin," *Journal of Geriatric Psychiatry and Neurology* 7 Suppl. 1 (October 1994): S 54–56. S. Bladt and H. Wagner, "Inhibition of MAO by Fractions of and Constituents of Hypericum Extract," *Journal of Geriatric Psychiatry and Neurology* 7 Suppl. 1 (October 1994): S 57–59.

12. B. Thiele, I. Brink, and M. Ploch, "Modulation of Cytokine Expression by Hypericum Extract," *Journal of Geriatric Psychiatry and Neurology* 7 Suppl. 1 (October 1994): S 60–62.

13. Vorbach et al., "Effectiveness and Tolerance of the Hypericum Extract LI 160."

CHAPTER 12. NUTRITIONAL HEALING I: SUPPLEMENTS

VITAMINS AND MINERALS

1. M. W. P. Carney et al., "Thiamine, Riboflavin and Pyridoxine Deficiency in Psychiatric Inpatients," *British Journal of Psychiatry* 141 (1982): 271–72.

2. J. W. Stewart et al., "Low B6 Levels in Depressed Outpatients," *Biological Psychiatry* 19, no. 4 (1984): 613–15.

3. Carney et al., "Thiamine, Riboflavin and Pyridoxine Deficiency." I. R. Bell et al., "Low Thyroxine Levels in Female Psychiatric Inpatients with Riboflavin Deficiency: Implications for Folate-Dependent Methylation," *Acta Psychiatrica Scandinavia* 85, no. 5 (May 1992): 360–63.

4. I. R. Bell et al., "Brief Communication. Vitamin B1, B2, and B6 Augmentation of Tricyclic Antidepressant Treatment in Geriatric Depression with Cognitive Dysfunction," *Journal of the American College of Nutrition* 11, no. 2 (April 1992): 159–63.

5. Stewart et al., "Low B6 Levels in Depressed Outpatients."

6. D. K. Zucker et al., "B12 Deficiency and Psychiatric Disorders: Case Report and Literature Review," *Biological Psychiatry* 16, no. 2 (1981): 197–205.

7. S. N. Young, "The Use of Diet and Dietary Components in the Study of Factors Controlling Affect in Humans: A Review," *Journal of Psychiatry and Neurosciences* 18, no. 5 (November 1993): 235–44.

8. Ibid. E. H. Reynolds et al., "Folate Deficiency in Depressive Illness," *British Journal of Psychiatry* 117 (1970): 287–92.

9. Young, "The Use of Diet."

10. I. R. Bell et al., "Vitamin B12 and Folate Status in Acute Geropsychiatric Inpatients: Affective and Cognitive Characteristics of a Vitamin Nondeficient Population," *Biological Psychiatry* 27, no. 2 (1990): 125–37.

11. G. J. Naylor and A. H. W. Smith, "Vanadium: A Possible Aetiological Factor in Manic Depressive Illness," *Psychological Medicine* 11 (1981): 249–56.

12. O. S. Brusov et al. "Thrombocytic Serotonergic Markers in Therapy-Resistant Patients with Endogenous Depression Undergoing Alpha-Tocopherol Treatment," *Zhurnal Nevropatologii I Psikhiatrii Imeni S. S. Korsakova* 95, no. 6 (1995): 72–76.

13. S. Hendler, *The Doctor's Vitamin and Mineral Encyclopedia* (New York: Simon and Schuster, 1990).

14. C. M. Banki et al., "Cerebrospinal Fluid Magnesium and Calcium Related to Amine Metabolites, Diagnosis, and Suicide Attempts," *Biological Psychiatry* 20, no. 2 (1985): 163–71. C. L. Bowden et al., "Calcium Function in Affective Disorders and Healthy Controls," *Biological Psychiatry* 23, no. 6 (1988): 367. S. R. Pliszka and G. A. Rogeness, "Calcium and Magnesium in Children with Schizophrenia and Major Depression," *Biological Psychiatry* 19, no. 6 (1984): 871–76.

15. Ibid. Hendler, *Doctor's Vitamin and Mineral Encyclopedia.*

16. M. F. McCarty, "Enhancing Central and Peripheral Insulin Activity as a Strategy for the Treatment of Endogenous Depression—An Adjuvant Role for Chromium Picolinate?" *Medical Hypotheses* 43, no. 4 (1994): 247–52.

17. W. C. Hawkes and L. Hornbostel, "Effects of Dietary Selenium on Mood in Healthy Men Living in a Metabolic Research Unit," *Biological Psychiatry* 39, no. 2 (1996): 121–28.

18. C. R. Hansen et al., "Copper and Zinc Deficiencies in Association with Depression and Neurological Findings," *Biological Psychiatry* 18, no. 3 (1983): 395–401. I. J. McLoughlin and J. S. Hodge, "Zinc in Depressive Disorder," *Acta Psychiatrica Scandinavia* 82 (December 1990): 451–53.

AMINO ACID THERAPY

19. H. Beckmann et al., "DL-Phenylalanine versus Imipramine: A Double-Blind Controlled Study," *Archiv Psychiatrie Nervenkrankheiten* 227, no. 1 (1979): 49–58.

20. H. Beckmann and E. Ludolph, "DL-Phenylalanine as an Antidepressant: Open Study," *Arzneimittel-Forschung* 28, no. 8 (1978): 1283–84.

21. H. M. Kravitz, H. C. Sabelli, and J. Fawcett, "Dietary Supplements of Phenylalanine and Other Amino Acid Precursors of Brain Neuroamines in the Treatment of Depressive Disorders," *Journal of the American Osteopathic Association* 84, no. 1, Suppl. (1984): 119–23.

22. J. Mann et al., "D-Phenylalanine in the Treatment of Endogenous Depression," *IRCS Journal of Medical Sciences* 8, no. 2 (1980): 116. H. Spatz et al., "Effects of D-Phenylalanine of Clinical Picture and Phenyethylaminuria in Depression," *Biological Psychiatry* 10, no. 2 (1975): 235–39.

23. A. J. Gelenberg et al., "Tyrosine for the Treatment of Depression," *American Journal of Psychiatry* 137, no. 5 (May 1980): 622–23. I. K. Goldberg, "L-Tyrosine in Depression," *Lancet,* August 16, 1980, p. 364. H. M. Van Praag, "Catecholamine Precursor Research in Depression: The Practical and Scientific Yield" in: *Amino Acids in Psychiatric Disease,* edited by M. A. Richardson (Washington, D.C.: American Psychiatric Press, 1990), pp. 77–98.

24. Ibid.

25. S. N. Young, "Factors Influencing the Therapeutic Effect of Tryptophan in Affective Disorders, Sleep, Aggression, and Pain," in Richardson, *Amino Acids in Psychiatric Disease,* pp. 49–76.

26. K. M. Bell et al., "S-Adenosylmethionine Treatment of Depression: A Controlled Clinical Trial," *American Journal of Psychiatry* 145, no. 9 (September 1988): 1110–14. A. Agnoli et al., "Effect of S-adenosyl-L-methionine (SAMe) Upon Depressive Symptoms," *Journal of Psychiatric Research* 13 (1976): 43–54.

THE THERAPEUTIC OILS

27. Calabrese Jr. et al. "Depression, Immunocompetence, and Prostaglandins of the E Series," *Psychiatry Research* 17 (1985): 41–47.

28. Y. H. Abdulla and K. Hamada, "Effect of ADP on PGE Formation in Blood Platelets from Patients with Depression, Mania, and Schizophrenia," *British Journal of Psychiatry* 127 (1975): 591–95.

29. S. Nishino et al., "Salivary Prostaglandin Concentrations: Possible State Indicators for Major Depression," *American Journal of Psychiatry* 146, no. 3 (1989): 365–68.

30. M. Blackburn, "Use of Efamol (Oil of Evening Primrose) for Depression and Hyperactivity in Children," in *Omega-6 Essential Fatty Acids: Pathophysiology and Roles in Clinical Medicine,* edited D. F. Horrobin (New York: Wiley-Liss, 1990).

31. P. O. Behan and M. H. Behan, "Essential Fatty Acids in the Treatment of Postviral Fatigue Syndrome," in Horrobin, *Omega-6 Essential Fatty Acids,* pp. 275–82.

32. M. J. Norden, *Beyond Prozac: Brain-Toxic Lifestyles, Natural Antidotes, and New Generation Antidepressants* (New York: HarperCollins, 1995).

CHAPTER 13. NUTRITIONAL HEALING II: FOOD AS MEDICINE

1. L. Christensen, A. Bourgeois, and R. Cockroft, "Dietary Alteration of Somatic Symptoms and Regional Brain Electrical Activity," *Biological Psychiatry* 29, no. 7 (1991): 679–82. L. Christensen and R. Burrows, "Dietary Treatment of Depression," *Behavioural Therapy* 21 (1990): 183–93. K. Krietsch, L. Christensen, and B. White, "Prevalence, Presenting Symptoms, and Psychological Characteristics of Individuals Experiencing a Diet-Related Mood Disturbance," *Behavioural Therapy* 19 (1988): 593–604.

2. M. S. Wallin and A. M. Rissanen, "Food and Mood: Relationship Between Food, Serotonin and Affective Disorders," *Acta Psychiatrica Scandinavia* Suppl. 377 (1994): 36–40.

3. R. J. Wurtman, "Nutrients Affecting Brain Composition and Behaviour," *Integrative Psychiatry* 5 (1987): 226–57.

4. G. Weidner et al., "Improvements in Hostility and Depression in Relation to Dietary Change and Cholesterol Lowering. The Family Heart Study," *Annals of Internal Medicine* 117, no. 10 (November 15, 1992): 820–23. R. B. Keith, K. A. O'Keefe, D. L. Blessing, and G. D. Wilson, "Alterations in Dietary Carbohydrate, Protein, and Fat Intake and Mood State in Trained Female Cyclists," *Medical Science in Sports and Exercise* 23, no. 2 (February 1991): 212–16.

5. For example, summarized in M. Gallerani et al., "Serum Cholesterol Concentrations in Parasuicide," *British Medical Journal* 310 (June 24, 1995): 1632–36.

6. C. J. Glueck et al., "Hypocholesterolemia and Affective Disorders," *American Journal of Medical Sciences* 308, no. 4 (October 1994): 218–25.

7. G. Engstrom et al., "Serum Lipids in Suicide Attempters," *Suicide and Life Threatening Behavior* 25, no. 3 (Fall 1995): 393–400. J. Wardle et al., "Randomised Placebo Controlled Trial of Effect on Mood of Lowering Cholesterol Concentration," *British Medical Journal* 313, no. 7049 (July 13, 1996): 75–78.

8. Weidner et al., "Improvements in Hostility."

9. J. J. Vitale, "Impact of Nutrition on Immune Function," in Vitale JJ and Broitman SA. *Advances in Human Clinical Nutrition* edited by J. J. Vitale and S. A. Broitman (Boston: John Wright, 1982), p. 93.

10. W. C. Willett, "Polyunsaturated Fat and the Risk of Cancer," *British Medical Journal* 311 (November 11, 1995): 1239–40.

11. H. C. Sabelli et al., "Clinical Studies on the Phenylethylamine Hypothesis of Affective Disorder: Urine and Blood Phenylacetic Acid and Phenylalanine Dietary Supplements," *Journal of Clinical Psychiatry* 47, no. 2 (February 1986): 66–70.

12. J. C. Newman and R. J. Holden, "The 'Cerebral Diabetes' Paradigm for Unipolar Depression," *Medical Hypotheses* 41, no. 5 (November 1993): 391–408.

13. I. R. Bell et al., "Depression and Allergies: Survey of a Nonclinical Population," *Psychotherapy and Psychosomatics* 55, no. 1 (1991): 24–31. A. Hoffer, "Allergy, Depression and Tricyclic Antidepressants," *Journal of Orthomolecular Psychiatry* 9, no. 3 (1980): 164–70.

14. P. S. Marshall, "Allergy and Depression: A Neurochemical Threshold Model of the Relation Between the Illnesses," *Psychological Bulletin* 113, no. 1 (January 1993): 23–43.

15. F. B. Michel, "Psychology of the Allergic Patient," *Allergy* 48, no. 18, Suppl. (1994): 28–30.

16. D. S. King, "Can Allergic Exposure Provoke Psychological Symptoms? A Double-Blind Test," *Biological Psychiatry* 16, no. 1 (1981): 3–19.

17. Hoffer, "Allergy."

18. G. J. Naylor and A. H. W. Smith, "Vanadium: A Possible Aetiological Factor in Manic-Depressive Illness," *Psychological Medicine* 11 (1981): 249–56.

19. C. Conri et al., "Does Vanadium Play a Role in Depressive States?" *Biological Psychiatry* 21, no. 5–6 (1986): 546–48. G. J. Naylor et al., "Tissue Vanadium Levels in Manic-Depressive Psychosis," *Psychological Medicine* 14 (1984): 767–72.

20. G. J. Naylor, "Vanadium and Affective Disorders," *Biological Psychiatry* 18, no. 1 (1983): 103–112. C. Conri et al., "Variations in Serum Vanadium Levels During the Treatment of Mental Depression," *Biological Psychiatry* 21, no. 13 (1986): 1335–39.

CHAPTER 14. ECOLOGY AND DEPRESSION

1. R. S. Schottenfeld and M. R. Cullen, "Organic Affective Illness Associated with Lead Intoxication," *American Journal of Psychiatry* 141, no. 11 (November 1984): 1423–26.

2. H. A. Waldron, *Lecture Notes on Occupational Medicine,* 3rd ed. (Oxford, England: Blackwell Scientific Publications, 1985), p. 14.

3. Schottenfeld and Cullen, "Organic Affective Illness."

4. J. B. Beaunder et al., "Short-Term Efficacy of Oral Dimer-catosuccinic Acid in Children with Low to Moderate Lead Intox-ication," *Pediatrics* 96 (October 1995): 683–87.

5. M. Murray and J. Pizzorno, *Encyclopedia of Natural Medicine* (London: McDonald and Co., 1990), p. 34.

6. R. L. Siblerud, J. Moti, and E. Kienholz, "Psychometric Evidence that Mercury from Silver Dental Fillings May Be an Etiological Factor in Depression, Excessive Anger, and Anxiety," *Psychological Reports* 74 (1994): 67–80.

7. D. W. Eggleston and M. Nylander, "Correlation of Dental Amalgam and Mercury in the Brain Tissue," *Journal of Prosthetic Dentistry* 58 (1987): 704–707.

8. Siblerud et al., "Psychometric Evidence."

9. M. L. Bleecker et al., "Dose-Related Subclinical Neurobehavioral Effects of Chronic Exposure to Low Levels of Organic Solvents," *American Journal of Industrial Medicine* 19, no. 6 (1991): 715–28. R. Kishi et al., "Neurobehavioral Effects of Chronic Occupational Exposure to Organic Solvents Among Japanese Industrial Painters," *Environmental Research* 62, no. 2 (August 1993): 303–313. G. Triebig et al., "Neuro-toxicity of Solvent Mixtures in Spray Painters. II. Neurologic, Psychiatric, Psychological, and Neuroradiologic Findings," *International Archives of Occupational and Environmental Health* 64, no. 5 (1992): 361–72.

10. L. A. Morrow, H. Kamis, and M. J. Hodgson, "Psychiatric Symptomatology in Persons with Organic Solvent Exposure," *Journal of Consulting and Clinical Psychology* 61, no. 1 (1993): 171–74. M. G. Cassitto et al., "Carbon Disulphide and the Central Nervous System: A 15-Year Neurobehavioural Surveillance of an Exposed Population," *Environmental Research* 63, no. 2 (November 1993): 252–63.

11. H. A. Waldron, *Lecture Notes on Occupational Medicine,* 3rd ed. (Oxford, England: Blackwell Scientific Publications, 1985), p. 48.

12. C. Poole et al., "Depressive Symptoms and Headaches in Relation to Proximity of Residence to an Alternating-Current Trans-mission Line Right-of-Way," *American Journal of Epidemiology* 137, no. 3 (February 1993): 318–30. S. Perry, L. Pearl, and R. Binns, "Power Frequency Magnetic Field; Depressive Illness and Myocardial Infarction," *Public Health* 103, no. 3 (May 1989): 177–80.

13. D. A. Savitz, C. A. Boyle, and P. Holmgreen, "Prevalence of Depression Among Electrical Workers," *American Journal of Industrial*

Medicine 25, no. 2 (February 1994): 165–76. S. McMahan, J. Ericson, and J. Meyer, "Depressive Symptomatology in Women and Residential Proximity to High-Voltage Transmission Lines," *American Journal of Epidemiology* 139, no. 1 (January 1994): 58–63.

14. M. Feychting and A. Ahlborn, "Magnetic Fields, Leukemia, and Central Nervous System Tumours in Swedish Adults Residing Near High-Voltage Power Lines," *Epidemiology* 5, no. 5 (September 1994): 501–509. D. A. Savitz and D. P. Loomis, "Magnetic Field Exposure in Relation to Leukemia and Brain Cancer Mortality Among Electric Utility Workers," *American Journal of Epidemiology* 141, no. 2 (January 1995): 123–34.

15. S. A. Stansfeld, "Noise, Noise Sensitivity and Psychiatric Disorder: Epidemiological and Psychophysiological Studies," *Psychological Medicine Monograph Supplement* 22 (1992): 1–44. S. Melamud, J. Luz, and M. S. Green, "Noise Exposure, Noise Annoyance and Their Relation to Psychological Distress, Accident and Sickness Absence Among Blue-Collar Workers—The Cordis Study," *Israeli Journal of Medical Sciences* 28, no. 8–9 (August-September 1992): 629–35. E. Ivanovich et al., "Noise Evaluation and Estimation of Some Specific and Non-Specific Health Indicators in Telephone Operators," *Reviews on Environmental Health* 10, no. 1 (January-March 1994): 39–46.

16. W. C. Sullivan and F. E. Kuo, "Urban Public Housing Residents and the Power of Trees," *Illinois Research,* Spring/Summer 1994.

CHAPTER 15. LIGHT

1. D. F. Kripke, "Controlled Trial of Bright Light for Nonseasonal Major Depressive Disorders," *Biological Psychiatry* 31, no. 2 (1992): 119–34. A. Mackert et al., "Phototherapy in Nonseasonal Depression," *Biological Psychiatry* 30, no. 3 (1991): 257–68.

2. B. W. Wilson, "Chronic Exposure to ELF Fields May Induce Depression," *Bioelectromagnetics* 9, no. 2 (1988): 195–205. K. P. Bhatnagar, "Comparative Morphology of the Pineal Gland," in *Biological Rhythms, Mood Disorders, Light Therapy, and the Pineal Gland,* edited by M. Shafii and S. L. Shaffii (Washington D.C.: American Psychiatric Press, 1990), pp. 3–38.

3. Ibid.

4. T. Partonen and M. Partinen, "Light Treatment for Seasonal Affective Disorder: Theoretical Considerations and Clinical Implications," *Acta Psychiatrica Scandinavia,* Suppl. 377 (1994): 41–45.

5. Ibid. and T. Partonen, "Effects of Morning Light Treatment on Subjective Sleepiness and Mood in Winter Depression," *Journal of Affective Disorders* 30, no. 2 (February 1994): 99–108.

6. M. J. Norden and D. H. Avery, "A Controlled Study of Dawn Simulation in Subsyndromal Winter Depression," *Acta Psychiatrica Scandinavia* 88, no. 1 (1993): 67–71.

7. K. Krauchi, A. Wirz-Justice, and P. Graw, "High Intake of Sweets Late in the Day Predicts Rapid and Persistent Response to Light Therapy in Winter Depression," *Psychiatry Research* 46, no. 2 (February 1993): 107–17. R. W. Lam, "Morning Light Therapy for Winter Depression: Predictors of Response," *Acta Psychiatrica Scandinavia* 89, no. 2 (February 1994): 97–101.

8. J. S. Carman et al., "Negative Effects of Melatonin on Depression," *American Journal of Psychiatry* 133 (October 1976): 1181–86. A. Wirz-Justice et al., "Morning or Night-Time Melatonin Is Ineffective in Seasonal Affective Disorder," *Journal of Psychiatric Research* 24, no. 2 (1990): 129–37.

CHAPTER 16. SLEEP

1. C. Guilleminault et al., "Nondrug Treatment Trials in Psychophysiologic Insomnia," *Archives of Internal Medicine* 155 (April 24, 1995): 838–44.

2. R. J. Reiter et al., "A Review of the Evidence Supporting Melatonin's Role as an Antioxidant," *Journal of Pineal Research* 18, no. 1 (1995): 1–11. T. M. Molis et al., "Melatonin Modulation of Estrogen-Related Proteins, Growth Factors, and Proto-Oncogenes in Human Breast Cancer," *Journal of Pineal Research* 18, no. 2 (1995): 93–103. I. V. Zhdanova, "Sleep-Inducing Effects of Low Doses of Melatonin Ingested in the Evening," *Clinical Pharmacology and Therapy* 57, no. 5 (May 1995): 552–58. D. Garfinkel et al., "Improvement of Sleep Quality in Elderly People by Controlled-Release Melatonin," *Lancet* 346, no. 8974 (August 26, 1995): 541–44. R. Nave, R. Peled, and P. Lavie, "Melatonin Improves Evening Napping," *European Journal of Pharmacology* 275 (1995): 213–16.

3. Nave et al., "Melatonin Improves Evening Napping." Garfinkel et al., "Improvement of Sleep Quality."

4. Zhdanova, "Sleep-Inducing Effects."

5. Nave et al., "Melatonin Improves Evening Napping."

6. J. S. Carman et al., "Negative Effects of Melatonin on Depression," *American Journal of Psychiatry* 133 (October 1976): 1181–86.

7. O. Lindahl and L. Lindwall, "Double Blind Study of a Valerian Preparation," *Pharmacology, Biochemistry and Behavior* 32, no. 4 (April 1989): 1065–66.

8. B. J. Spring et al., "Effects of Protein and Carbohydrate Meals on Mood and Performance: Interactions with Sex and Age," *Journal of Psychiatric Research* 17: 155–67.

9. M. Taylor, "Insomnia and Nutrition [Letter]," *Australian Family Physician* 23, no. 3 (March 1994): 498.

CHAPTER 17. MOTION AND RELAXATION

1. E. W. Martinsen, "Physical Activity and Depression: Clinical Experience," *Acta Psychiatrica Scandinavia* Suppl. 377 (1994): 23–27. J. H. Greist, "Exercise Intervention with Depressed Outpatients," in *Exercise and Mental Health*, edited by W. P. Morgan and S. E. Goldston (New York: Hemisphere Publishing, 1987), pp. 117–22. D. V. Harris, "Comparative Effectiveness of Running Therapy and Psychotherapy," Morgan and Goldston, *Exercise and Mental Health*, pp. 123–29. W. E. Sime, "Exercise in the Prevention and Treatment of Depression," in Morgan and Goldston, *Exercise and Mental Health*, pp. 145–52.

2. Martinsen, "Physical Activity and Depression."

3. B. G. Berger and D. R. Owen, "Mood Alteration with Yoga and Swimming: Aerobic Exercise May Not Be Necessary," *Perceptual and Motor Skills* 75, no. 3, Pt. 2 (December 1992): 1331–43.

CHAPTER 18. THOUGHT

1. A. O'Leary, "Stress, Emotion, and Human Immune Function," *Psychological Bulletin* 108, no. 3 (1990) 363–82.

2. Ibid.

3. A. T. Beck and A. J. Rush, "Cognitive Therapy," in Kaplan HI, and Sadock BJ. (eds.) *Comprehensive Textbook of Psychiatry VI*, Vol. 2, 6th ed., edited by H. I. Kaplan and B. J. Sadock (Baltimore: Williams and Wilkins, 1995), pp. 1847–57.

4. Adapted from C. F. Newman and A. T. Beck, "Cognitive Therapy of Affective Disorders," in *Depressive Disorders: Facts, Theories, and*

Treatment Methods, edited by B. B. Wolman and G. Stricker (New York: John Wiley and Sons, 1990), pp. 343–67.

5. Ibid.

6. Adapted from I. M. Blackburn and K. M. Davidson, *Cognitive Therapy for Depression and Anxiety: A Practitioner's Guide* (Oxford, England: Blackwell Scientific Publications, 1990).

INDEX

✦

About the Author

✦

Jonathan Zuess, M.D., is a physician who has trained in both conventional and alternative medicines. His interest in natural medicine is a family tradition, stretching back many generations. After completing medical school and doing an internship in conventional medicine and a residency in psychiatry, he studied a number of alternative therapies. He is a member of the American Holistic Medical Association. He is also an avid backpacker and has spent several months exploring remote wilderness areas in Australia. He practices in Arizona.